THE GOSPEL
AND CHRISTIAN EDUCATION

Books by
D. CAMPBELL WYCKOFF
Published by The Westminster Press

THE TASK OF CHRISTIAN EDUCATION
THE GOSPEL AND CHRISTIAN EDUCATION

THE GOSPEL
AND
CHRISTIAN
EDUCATION

A Theory of Christian Education for Our Times

by

D. Campbell Wyckoff

Philadelphia

THE WESTMINSTER PRESS

Library of Congress Catalog Card No. 59–5128

PRINTED IN THE UNITED STATES OF AMERICA

Contents

Preface

The problems that confront Christian education in Protestant churches are of many kinds. Some of them are practical problems involving objectives, administration, and curriculum. A great deal of creative work has been done on such problems, but there is evidence that solving them will not be a short-term matter.

The most critical problem that faces Christian education, however, is its need to understand itself — to gain deep insight into what it is about. It needs to see how it is related to the cultural situation, to the church's life and thought, and to the educational process. This problem of self-understanding is the problem of theory.

Building a theory of Christian education for Protestantism is a matter of the discovery and refinement of a body of basic principles that will give Protestants a clear idea of what Christian education is concerned with, and will provide the guidance needed for the practical aspects of the church's work in objectives, curriculum, and administration. This body of principles must be of such a character that it will be basic to everything the church does in its educational work. In particular, it must be both theologically valid and educationally sound.

The present volume is intended to be an introduction

7

to the study of theory in Christian education. While the point of view that I developed in popular fashion in *The Task of Christian Education* (The Westminster Press, 1955) is more systematically stated in this book, the formulation of a point of view has been only one of my purposes. The other emphasis here is on theory and theorizing. Thus the second, and perhaps in the long run the more important, objective of the book is to propose a way of constructing a theory of Christian education, a way of theorizing about our task.

What the reader will find here, then, is an exposition of my point of view used to illustrate the way in which I believe a point of view is to be built. This, I hope, is only the beginning of an exploration that will lead me and many others a long way farther on toward the building of a thoroughgoing and sound body of principles and practice in Christian education. I can think of nothing that is more sorely needed in our field at the present time.

Three aspects of the construction of theory are explored. The first is the proper use of the foundation disciplines. The next is the nature and functions of theory in education and in Christian education. Finally, in view of the nature and functions of theory, concentration is focused on objectives, curriculum principles, and principles of administration.

While my former book was intended for all who are engaged in Christian education, this one is intended primarily for those who are concerned with its theoretical aspects — professors and students in Christian education, ministers and directors of Christian education, program people, and writers and editors. Others may find it valuable, but it is written chiefly for persons at the policy and planning level.

It would be literally impossible for me to indicate all the people to whom I am indebted in this writing. All those who have taught me would, if they were to read this volume, see evidences of their handiwork (though I hasten to add that they need not assume responsibility for the material in the form I have given it). In this connection I think particularly of what it has meant to study with Paul M. Limbert, the late Herman Harrell Horne, the late Samuel L. Hamilton, and Louise Antz. For several years I was a member of a remarkable committee, the National Council of Churches' Committee on Senior High Objectives. The penetrating new look that this committee took at Christian education has probably been the greatest stimulus to pursuing a study of theory at this time. I am deeply grateful to Ray L. Henthorne, the chairman, to the other members of the committee, and to the National Council of Churches, not only for the inestimable help they have given me, but also for permission to draw freely from the work that we have done together. Rowena Ferguson, with whom I was associated in the Senior High study, read the entire manuscript and made important suggestions that improved the style and helped to clarify the key ideas. Neil R. Paylor, Teaching Fellow in Christian Education at Princeton Theological Seminary, helped to prepare the index. Many others, co-workers and students, have assisted and encouraged in various important ways. Princeton Theological Seminary and its president, John A. Mackay, have provided exactly the freedom and resources that have been necessary for this work.

The reader will become aware that more detailed studies are needed in the use of the foundation disciplines, in objectives, in curriculum, and in administration. I hope to follow this book in due time with such studies.

RATIONALE FOR A THEORY
OF CHRISTIAN EDUCATION

[1]
The Process and Condition
of Culture

CAN a sound Protestant theory of education be built today? Of the many important factors to be considered in answering this question the key factor is that of modern culture, its nature, influence, and the direction of its development.

The church is deeply affected by the cultural situation. Its life takes on the character of its day, even when it tries most assiduously to avoid it, and its theology tends to speak the language of the day. At the same time, the church is concerned with the culture in a creative way. It has a mission to the culture of the day that is critical, constructive, and reconstructive. The church always reflects and remakes the culture in which it lives.

Because Christian education is one of the chief functions of the church, the educational ministry being in and of the church, it too is influenced by the culture. In fact, as the cultural situation affects the church and through it its educational work, so also the cultural situation affects educational procedures and institutions, which are in turn mirrored in the church's educational work. Thus Christian education reflects the culture in which it lives.

But Christian education is also concerned with the culture creatively. As the church tries faithfully to pursue its mission to the modern world, among its most useful means for criticism of prevailing cultures, for the building of culture, and for cultural reconstruction, are its educational programs and institutions. Thus Christian education participates in rebuilding the culture in which it lives.

We begin by looking at the cultural process and the cultural situation. This is followed by a consideration of education in the light of its cultural foundations. Then we turn to the church, the mutual influence of the culture and the church's theology, the mutual influence of the culture and the church's life and work, and the role of Christian education as the church's teaching ministry.

THE CULTURAL PROCESS

A simple but accurate theory of culture provides the basis that is needed for understanding and interpreting the cultural process. Fortunately such a theory is available and is authoritatively established.

This theory of culture may be stated in several propositions: The development of culture is the way a society makes something of its life. It is the embodiment of the way it sees life in a way of life. It is the way in which a society orders its corporate existence. It consists of a society's accepted values, and the modes by which it expresses those values.

Using such a theory for understanding and interpreting the cultural process, we can easily see what a society does about the questions of the meaning and conduct of life that keep cropping up. The culture answers those questions by developing customs, folklore, cult, and doctrine, all of which express and exalt what society has found to be valuable and worth conserving. Its customs, folklore, cult, and doctrine also perform the function of helping society to avoid what it has come to feel is worthless or dangerous.

The pieces and fragments of existence have to be put together. A generation takes what it is given, what happens to it, and what it is, looks at these ingredients, and out of them builds its life. It thus uses and creates. Its motive and impetus is the need for coming to terms with life, for arriving at a *modus vivendi*.

One of the virtues of such a theory of culture is that it gives us an explanation for the varieties of cultures that we confront. Some generations have their way of life given to them — they inherit their culture. Other generations have their way of life forced on them — they submit to cultural pressures. A way of life has been given to some generations that has to be patched up in order to make it suitable for their time — they reconstruct their culture. Still other generations have to build a new way of life almost from scratch — they have to create their culture.

Another of the virtues of such a theory of culture is that it provides the data for understanding the phenomena of cultural conflicts. As two or more cultures come into contact with each other, their interrelationships run the gamut from elimination of opposition (or, less frequently, cultural withdrawal), through exploitation of one another, equilibrium, and coalescence, to assimilation. This continuum represents the range of possible cultural conflict and competition. (See Jessie Barnard, *American Community Behavior;* The Dryden Press, Inc., 1949.)

A third virtue in such a theory of culture is that it enables us to see the functions of various aspects of human life (religion and education among them) in proper relation to one another. Some of the aspects of human life that thus come into clear relation to one another are language, the community, the home, philosophy, the sciences, religion, and education.

Language is understood, within this theory of culture, as one of the most telling expressions of culture (in fact, one of its art forms) , and also as the most broadly effective medium for the communication of the culture to its on-coming members and to its neighbors.

The community is regarded as the social organism that not only sustains culture but creates it. This theory of culture thus focuses attention upon the analysis of the foundations of community life and behavior.

The home is seen as conveying to its children a way of life which the parents deeply feel and believe in, and which is so much a part of the atmosphere in which the child grows up that its imparting is scarcely a conscious process. The absence of any such cultural orientation for the home is considered to be the chief cause of various kinds of social disorganization beyond the home, juvenile delinquency being one form of such disorganization.

Philosophy is considered as the highest intellectual function of the culture, as it puts its basic perceptions of itself and its environment to work in the answering of the fundamental questions of existence.

The sciences, in this theory of culture, are thought of as the culture's attempt, using its basic perceptions as in philosophy, to probe the nature of its life and existence, and to apply the results of such investigation to the reordering and betterment of its life. The natural sciences probe one side of the culture's existence, and the social sciences the other.

Religion is the view and appreciation of what is highest and most valuable that permeates thought and feeling and guides and motivates human behavior. It permeates the thought and feeling not only of the individual but also of the group, and thus becomes the most telling aspect of the culture. It is concerned with ultimate meaning and with ultimate power. This is made clear in the distinction that is drawn between magic and religion. The function of magic in society is to seek to control ultimate power and to bend it to man's will. This is done by using the charm, the spell, and other means. The " superstitions of religion " are not really religious, but magical. The function of religion in society is to seek to relate to ultimate power and find ways by which man may bend his will to it. This is done through worship, commitment, group membership, and other means. It is easy to see how religion performs a culturally conservative function (enabling a culture to hold firmly to its values and way of life) , while it also performs a culturally reconstructive function (enabling a culture to form new values and adopt a new way of life) .

The priest usually symbolizes the conservative role of religion in culture, dealing as he does primarily with the cultic side of religion, its design, symbolism, places of worship, modes of worship, and modes of religious behavior. The prophet usually symbolizes the culturally reconstructive role of religion in culture, dealing as he does primarily with the reassessment of cult, the personal aspects of faith, and the ethical implications of religion in culture. The theologian performs the intellectual function of religion in culture, interpreting and reinterpreting its essential meaning so that it may be understood and responded to by each new generation and by various cultures as they change. Depending upon circumstances, the theologian's emphasis is more or less priestly, or more or less prophetic. Religion may thus be said to be sometimes the conserver of culture and sometimes the reformer of culture.

In V. Ogden Vogt's *Cult and Culture* (The Macmillan Company, 1951) religion is described as the chief source of social culture, and cult (the system of activities which

comprise public worship) as the aspect of religion that develops the inner spiritual order that is necessary for social
cohesion. The power of cult, according to this view, is to
be found in the facts that (1) the ritual acts of the cult
have or are thought to have actual objective practical ef-
fects, (2) in the cult all the factors of man's life are sur-
veyed for appraisal and relative arrangement, (3) it is by
and through cult that religious ideas and moral ideals are
given popular force and currency, (4) it is enjoyed, having
an effect of personal fulfillment and of social wholeness,
and (5) it is itself a spiritual order, its intellectual, moral,
and esthetic components harmonized, thus producing for
the individual that inner spiritual order which is necessary
to outer political order. Vogt helps us to see the relation
of religion to several of the other aspects of human culture
in a paragraph in which he puts religion at the center of
the theory of culture that we have been discussing:

> " In any society, the philosophies of the scholar and the
> seer become the moralities of commerce only when
> passed through the alembic of the arts of public worship.
> The traits and customs of societal culture, even those
> seemingly remote from religion, are to some degree
> touched by the outlooks and preferences, the ideals and
> values celebrated in the religious cult. Social religion
> gathers up and popularizes the meanings of science and
> philosophy, specifies the rights and wrongs of conduct,
> and upholds the ultimate conceptions reflected in the
> images of the arts. The culture of society is derived
> primarily from the cult of religion." (Used by permis-
> sion of The Macmillan Company.)

In all its complexity, then, the cultural process clearly
involves in an integral way the functions of language and
the arts, the community, the home, philosophy, the sciences,
and religion. The functions of education in culture will

be dealt with in the next chapter, but it can be indicated briefly that education's function in relation to the culture involves planned encounter, nurture, critical analysis, and guidance toward cultural reconstruction.

A fourth virtue of the theory of culture that we have been considering is that it enables us to give proper place to the individual. In a sense the individual is the creation of culture. Some cultures do not give rise to the free, independent self. Western culture has characteristically done so.

The individual in Western culture stands in an independent relation to the culture that has shaped and molded him. He is in constant encounter with it, but that encounter is critical as well as receptive. In a sense, this is why Western man has a profound feeling of alienation, why he tends to exalt searching for truth over the discovery of truth, why he is obsessed with reviewing and changing his way of life, and why consequently his culture has become so complex. In a sense, too, this is why he is so often lonely and isolated, possessed of no satisfying bond with his fellows.

While fully acknowledging man's dependence upon culture, the theory of culture that we have been examining also recognizes that the individual in critical encounter with culture is likely to ask: " What is going on around here? How in the world did I get here? What is happening to me? "

The individual watches things shape themselves around him, mold themselves, and take on new forms and patterns. His very perceiving of them is part of the process of their formation and change. He participates in the shaping, the molding, and the making of new forms and patterns. But even as he watches and participates he may ask: " But why am I here? Why am I thus? Why am I not elsewhere and otherwise? Who would I be, and what would I be, if I were elsewhere and otherwise? " Kingsley's Alexander Hamilton reflects before the duel on the " strange destiny " that has driven him to build a political system that has become something he no longer believes in. Newman, seeking enlightenment, even enough enlightenment to see one step ahead, acknowledges that he " was not ever thus." Abraham set out to seek a city, and Moses a Promised Land. Paul became a new man in Christ.

The theory of culture that interprets it as society's way of making something of its life, as the embodiment of its view of life in a way of life, as the way in which a society orders its corporate existence, and as consisting of a society's accepted values and the modes by which it expresses those values — this theory of culture is at its best as it deals with the individual and his meaning. There is no lack of consistency with its fundamental social orientation when it describes the individual as emerging within culture, responding to it, reacting to it, and in the process either becoming what it intends him to be or, together with his fellows, trying to remake it into a more fitting social means for the meeting of his needs and the expression of his values. The individual is nurtured, responds, reacts, becomes, and creates within a situation of cultural variety and conflict, and within a situation in which culture takes particular forms of language, community life, home life, philosophical explanations, scientific investigations, religion, and education. It is within the particular cultural situation that the individual confronts that he and his society come to terms with life, arrive at a way of life, and thus adopt or create a culture.

Out of the complexity of culture, then, this theory of

culture gives us a valuable key to understanding the various facets of the cultural problem. It promises real assistance in dealing with Protestant education, since it puts the functions of religion and education so clearly into focus, and relates them so carefully to the other significant aspects of human life and endeavor.

The real value of this understanding of the cultural process becomes evident as it is used in the analysis of our present cultural situation, since it is the culture in which we live that presents us with our peculiar problems in religion and education.

The Cultural Situation

Drawing from the theory of culture that has just been considered, we see that a particular culture may be analyzed and understood if the inquirer can get reliable answers to four questions about it:

1. Upon what basic foundations and values are the members of the culture agreed?
2. What is their way of life?
3. What authority do they generally acknowledge?
4. What is the source of their hope?

The nature of our cultural situation will become fairly evident as we discover the answers that are now given to these questions. Then we will be able to see how the cultural situation in which we live conditions Protestant education, and how Protestant education may meet the situation.

However, before attempting to pinpoint answers to these questions, let us take a broad and rather random look at the world we live in and see what some of the manifestations of our culture are. This calls for a brief look at its view of nature, the world scene, the national scene, the community, the church, the home, the personal outlook of its members, and the historical outlook of its members. Such a broad and random look may provide the data from which to draw answers on its foundations and values, its way of life, its acknowledged authority, and its source of hope.

Man has achieved in our time a mastery of what seems to be one of the basic powers of inanimate nature. He has already used that mastery for a destructive purpose that is beyond anything heretofore known, but has only begun to use it for constructive purposes. Even as he propels himself along in his mastery of nature, his spirit trembles with fear. As Romana Guardini has pointed out in *The End of the Modern World* (Sheed & Ward, Inc., 1956), modern man has lost significant contact with nature — he is not refreshed by the world of nature. He has departed from the great traditions and is obsessed with a technology that he cannot tame. Modern man lives in a secular world in which he is seeking power, but is losing " his own position in the realm of being." This is our contact with nature.

A look at the world scene shows up various communistic and fascistic totalitarianisms, a defensive spirit among the democracies, East-West tension and conflict, the formation of political blocs, the cold war, diplomacy by propaganda, the presence and fear of highly destructive weapons, racial and religious conflict, resurgent nationalism, the manipulation of small nations by the larger powers, cynicism in human relations, and an assumption that the good life can be organized into existence.

There is, on the other hand, the side of the world scene that comprises technological advance and attention to underdeveloped areas, the speeding up of communications and facility of contact throughout the world (especially between East and West), the vision of one world and the struggle for world order, freedom for formerly subject people and a new dignity for little nations, a people's courage in the face of literally insuperable odds, a situation in which the power of the weapons in hand has made the great nations fearful of their use, speedy diplomacy, an effective international organization, voluntary groups that are willing to investigate and act on matters of international concern, and access to competent analysts of the world situation. This is what a glance at the world scene reveals.

A look at the national scene shows up the omnipresence of change, the urbanization and sophistication of the people, the mobility of population, artificial social distinctions, race prejudice, religious tensions (Protestant, Catholic, Jew, and secularist), a slackening of moral values (dishonesty in high places, gambling and vice, the excessive use of liquor, the selfish use of sex, the rise of crime and juvenile delinquency, and waste of natural resources), mass culture and spectator culture, the molding of public opinion by advertising, mental illness, chauvinism and a misunderstanding of democracy, mass democracy, subversion, obsession with security, political irresponsibility, lobbying and self-seeking by pressure groups, national hysteria over communism, isolationism, militarism, bureaucracy and the welfare state, and the assumption of the efficacy of organization (dependence upon committees, officers, regulations, directives, and endless meetings). The other side of the national picture involves a high standard of living, a stable social and economic order, a general spirit of good will, a concern for public education and higher education, a concern for human welfare and the rights of special groups, concern for the conservation of natural resources, competent and statesmanlike political leaders, assumption of a responsible world role, and the growth and use of the social sciences. This is what a glance at the national scene reveals.

At this point, enough data have been accumulated so that a guess may be hazarded as to the answers to the four questions that will reveal the heart of our culture. Then these answers may be further checked with data on the community, the church, the home, the personal outlook of the people, and their historical outlook:

1. *Upon what basic foundations and values are the members of the culture agreed?* In a deeply pervasive sense, none. Yet there are foundations and values that are agreed upon by various groups within the culture. What we have, then, is not so much a culture as a plurality of cultures.

2. *What is their way of life?* Once the fact of cultural pluralism is taken into account, our culture's way of life appears to be twofold: the dynamic search for unity of spirit, and in its absence the building of a social structure that can hold things together, thus necessarily highly complex.

3. *What authority do they generally acknowledge?* The only authority generally acknowledged is that of man — secular human authority.

4. *What is their source of hope?* This is revealed in the resource that all turn to and use in their planning for the betterment of the human lot. That resource is science.

Our culture, then, may be characterized as pluralistic, dynamic, complex, secular, and scientific.

Testing this conclusion in terms of its applicability to the community, the church, the home, the personal outlook of members of the culture, and the historical outlook they have, we see almost immediately that it is accurate.

In the community the social class structure is based upon such variables as position and prestige, occupation, possessions, types of social interaction, class consciousness and political ideology, and value orientation. (See Joseph A. Kahl, *The American Class Structure;* Rinehart & Company, Inc., 1957.) Yet the community performs its essential functions in meeting the needs of its people, and at the present time provides services in most cases far in excess of their basic needs.

The church is interested in having an effective program and in reaching the people. Its efforts along these lines run the whole gamut from the radical reformulation of doctrine (both in obscurantist and in liberal directions), through concentrated efforts to be functional, to the use of the various media of mass persuasion that the secular world has invented. Yet in spite of such confusion, the church continues to proclaim the gospel and to carry out Christ's ministry.

The modern home has ceased to be primarily organic, a condition in which mutual dependence, direction, and support were its chief notes, and has become atomistic, a condition in which the major concern of each member is with himself and his individual interests and problems. The home is thus used by its members for their private benefit, rather than being the fellowship to which each contributes his best efforts. Yet even now the home remains the warmest and closest human fellowship. In recent times it has again come into its own in fulfilling its procreative function. Furthermore, the sacrifice of parents for the welfare and advancement of their children is incalculable.

The personal outlook of the members of the culture includes the romantic, the morally relativistic, and the
philosophically confused. They seek escape through sex,
travel, and other means. They tend to distrust the human
intellect. Their character is reflected in their literature
and arts, which express various degrees of cynicism, senti-
mentalism, and genuine search for values. The fact of
abnormality and mental illness, symptomatic of their cultural confusion, and the inadequacy of their prevailing
operative values, is contrasted with their ideal of a normal
individual in a normal world: a person who holds worthy
ideals, thinks straight, has the ability to love, lives a clean
life, and is socially responsible. In spite of their distrust
of the human intellect, there is an almost strained effort to
cultivate intellectual humility, receptivity, cultural rich-
ness, morality, and personal discipline. There is a recognition that the responsibilities of modern men and women
in this automated-atomic age call for systematic self-
discipline, so that the chosen or assigned job may be suf-
ficiently and expertly done. This is not a careless age —
men and women will dedicate years of their lives to the
systematic cultivation of needed professional skills. The
businessman, the scientist, the engineer, the architect, the
teacher, the minister must master their skills of mind and
hand if they are to contribute anything to society and the
community.

The historical outlook of the members of the culture is
dominated by their expectations from the results of scientific research and planning. It is almost exclusively oriented to the future. Any orientation to the past seems
affected and anachronistic. In answer to the question of
where we are heading, a group of scientists recently produced a study whose main results were summarized in
these paragraphs:

" In the next hundred years the earth's population will multiply at least two to four times. Technology can feed, clothe, and shelter these people adequately, and in some cases well.

" There will be no shortage of minerals, meals, or metals. Machine civilization will spread over the earth, and it can provide for all from the most common substances: air, sea water, ordinary rock, and sunlight.

" Only one possible raw material shortage is foreseen — brain power. Educated men and women are needed to plan and design, to construct and operate the machine civilization that will care for the startling increase in world population expected by the year 2050." (*The New York Times,* May 21, 1956. Used by permission. See Harrison Brown, James Bonner, and John Weir, *The Next Hundred Years;* The Viking Press, Inc., 1957.)

Science thus predicts the future and sets its own conditions for its achievement. It does this in spite of the threats to human life that it has itself produced.

Even such a cursory survey as this is enough to indicate what kind of cultural situation we have to deal with at present. It is pluralistic in that there are no generally agreed on foundations and values undergirding it. It is dynamic, however, since it is in search of such foundations and values. Because this search for unity of spirit is far from consummation, the fabric of society is held together by a highly complex organizational structure, a sort of culture-substitute which perhaps should be recognized realistically as all the common culture we have. The very fact of this complex organizational structure as the symbol of our culture makes it clear why as far as we have a prevailing authority it is secular, and why as far as we have a prevailing hope it lies in science.

This is not a situation to be bewailed. It is a situation to be seen for what it is, and dealt with for what it is. The theory that sees culture as society's way of hammering out a way of life through gaining and expressing adequate fundamental values makes it clear how powerful and enduring this and any other culture is in the lives of its members. It is in terms of this culture that education's work is done. It is within the context of this culture that the church of Jesus Christ seeks to minister.

We turn next, then, to an attempt to understand education in the light of its cultural foundations. After that, we will be in a position to consider the church and its educational work.

[2]

Education in Our Culture

How does education — not necessarily Christian education, for the moment, but education in general — do its work in a culture like ours?

The cultural process is the way in which a society orders its corporate existence; it consists of a society's accepted values, and the modes by which it expresses those values. Our culture orders its existence in a pluralistic, but dynamic and highly complex, way; its values are predominantly secular and scientific.

EDUCATION AND CULTURE

Education is the bridge between a culture and the new supplies of persons that its society keeps producing. Human society is constantly renewed by the birth of new persons within it, and those persons need to be educated.

Look at the individual person for a moment. He is an organism with an unusual endowment: he can perceive and know — he has a mind; he can feel, appreciate, and identify — he has spirit. He is an organism that grows: he accumulates size and gains proportion — it takes him about fifteen years to grow up; his growth is continuous and sequential — gradually he undertakes more and more difficult tasks through which, as they build one on the other, he develops as a person. He is a member of the hu-

man race: he cannot live without other human beings; he
is an integral part of the human community; he grows
within a given culture, according to a given way of life;
he is subject to all the capacities and abilities as well as the
limitations and disabilities of being human. He is an individual: he needs and demands personal integrity; he
needs to strike a balance between the objective and subjective aspects of experience, between his encounter with
reality (objectivity) and how he feels about it (subjectiv-
ity) ; he needs an orientation outside himself to save him
from slavery to self, society, and culture.

Obviously, it is the function of the culture to provide a
context of meaning within which the individual may
realize himself. This it does by providing him with customs, folklore, cult, and doctrine. The culture is thus the
chief means for the individual's achieving the perspective
on life that he needs.

Look now at the culture's educational function in dealing with the individual. The continuity of human existence through the generations depends upon the perpetuation and growth of human culture. The members of each
new generation are expected to grow to responsible maturity through adopting and re-creating the culture of the
preceding generations. Each generation thus makes the
culture its own, retaining what is essential and valuable,
and effecting such changes as become necessary and desirable. In this process not only does education take place,
but cultures themselves develop, are maintained, and decline.

The major process implied in the perpetuation and
growth of human culture is learning: the learning of such
things as information, skills, ideas, and attitudes. The
older generation seeks to guide the learning process and

therefore establishes and maintains certain agencies of education: home education, community schooling, church education, and many others.

The editor of *The Christian Century* put this matter brilliantly in this amusing piece:

" Most New Yorkers didn't notice it, but one alert reporter did. During the recent wildcat strike that tied up the subways just at rush hour, the hurried, harried millions pushed down the long stairs to the silent underground stations, were turned away at the toll gates, and then pressed back upstairs to seek some surface transportation. No one in the ascending stream told anyone in the descending stream on the same staircase that it was pointless to go all the way down. And none of those going down asked anyone going up why they were so suddenly turned around. To have communicated so, commented the reporter, would have violated New York's unwritten law that no one speaks to anyone. So the morose masses slogged through the same mistake, million by millon. Almost you can see the generations of men stumbling down the long staircases of history, coming to impasse, seeking other solutions — and volunteering far too little of their knowledge and wisdom to those who follow, repeating old mistakes. Scholars write books, scientists leave records, the church makes creeds, and all these should be the voice of those who have gone the distance to those who could get farther and go faster if they didn't have to push on into all the same blind alleys. But for the testimony to be telling, those who are on the way back must speak up to those who are on the way in. And those who are going down will do well to ask questions and listen sharply to those who are coming up." (*The Christian Century*, July 4, 1956. Copyright, 1956, Christian Century Foundation. Reprinted by permission.)

EDUCATION IN A UNIFIED CULTURE

Education takes place most easily in a culture that has unity based upon certain common assumptions about the meaning of existence and whose way of life is an expression of those assumptions. In such a setting all education, including education in religion and values, takes place as these common assumptions about the meaning of existence and the way of life that expresses them are passed on from generation to generation in cult and doctrine. This is seldom institutionalized; it is largely informal.

The culture is thus transmitted by its society to each new generation in relatively unstructured ways. Eugene A. Nida has analyzed this type of education and contrasted it with modern Western education in his book *Customs and Cultures* (Harper & Brothers, 1954) :

> " For us, the word ' education ' means the classroom, probably the most artificial technique ever devised for conveying instruction. It is entirely too easy to lose sight of the fact that other societies educate their children, even though they do not have formal schools. Children are taught fishing, hunting, housebuilding, tribal lore — all in the natural surroundings of meaningful activity. . . . In many primitive cultures children participate much more in the activities of the community than they do in ours. . . . Children generally have much more of a sense of being wanted and of belonging. . . .
>
> " The capacity which all cultures possess for molding individuals to fit the cultural pattern is truly remarkable. With little formal regimentation and often without any corporal punishment, societies not only teach necessary skills but inculcate concepts of loyalty, responsibility, and for the most part complete agreement with the moral order of the culture in question." (Used by permission of the publisher.)

EDUCATION IN MORE COMPLEX CULTURES

As Nida's comments indicate, education's ways become more complicated in situations of cultural differentiation. Society proceeds quite understandably to perpetuate its modes of differentiation as part of its way of life, and schools the young in them. As specific subcultures develop, society's ways of educating become more and more complex and institutionalized. The educational bridge becomes more difficult to design, construct, and maintain.

Our culture — pluralistic, dynamic, complex, secular, and scientific — seeks for the meaning of existence through philosophies constructed on the basis of scientific investigations. Its way of life is also scientific, and is "in the making." In the process of conducting the scientific investigations that it needs for its philosophy and its life, it has uncovered a great deal of information about human nature, human development, personality, learning, and the functions of social groups and movements.

This has shown our culture how to conduct the educational enterprise that it needs. A science of education has begun to emerge. (Scientific knowledge along these lines is, in fact, so far advanced that it permits, in diabolical hands, the phenomenon of brainwashing.) This science of education is in many respects highly technical, requiring professional training for those engaged in using it. Highly organized institutions have been set up to take over the work of education, and now serve the people on a mass basis. These schools have to be geared to a professional level of service because they try to base their work on the emerging science of education.

Thus, while education takes place within a unified culture in relatively informal ways, in our heterogeneous culture it has tended to become an institutionalized science.

Education and Culture in History

Our present educational situation may be seen from another perspective — the historical. A very brief look at the history of education will assist us to see how our current educational program has developed.

Educational theorists until the end of the Middle Ages concentrated on what was to be taught; how teaching was to be done was more or less incidental. True, Socrates used a method — but it amounted to intelligent conversation. Aristotle's method was peripatetic, which is to say that it was so taken for granted that a mannerism was the only thing noteworthy about it. Socrates, through Plato, was interested in developing a curriculum for the various strata of an ideally organized society. Aristotle was interested in an exhaustive cataloguing of the universe, so that it might be understood and handled well by each succeeding generation.

Hebrew education, when it was not carried out informally in the home, consisted of the drumming in of history and morality, together with a method that boiled down to debate and argumentation.

The education of the Middle Ages is symbolized by the refinement of the seven liberal arts (the arts appropriate to the free man). The church was in this period so completely dominant that it had nothing to fear, it felt, from their development and use. The seven liberal arts consisted of the trivium (the three elementary liberal arts): grammar, rhetoric, and logic; and the quadrivium (the four higher liberal arts): arithmetic, geometry, astronomy, and music. The prevailing method of education was simply that of association with a teacher and listening to his lectures.

In our day — that is, since the end of the Middle Ages — three significant developments have taken place. First, the arts have tended to become subordinated to the expanding sciences, so that we hear currently a great deal about the "defense of the humanities." Secondly, concentration has centered more and more on how education takes place rather than upon the subject matter of which it consists. This has accompanied the rapid expansion of the educational establishment, and has been the major concern of such educational theorists as Comenius (who advocated realistic contact with the environment), Pestalozzi (who built on the idea of observation), Herbart (whose theory was used as a basis for the famous series of steps through which it was thought anything could be learned), Froebel (who used symbols as the basis for education), Dewey (who stressed learning through problem-solving), Thorndike (to whom we owe the so-called "laws of learning" — readiness, exercise, and effect), and the perceptionists (whose theory is that learning depends mainly upon insight). Thirdly, public education has become universal on the elementary and secondary levels, and is fast becoming so in higher education. This has been accompanied by a burgeoning establishment devoted to professional training.

The history of education thus reveals a trend toward an education that is very self-conscious so far as methodology is concerned. A pluralistic and dynamic culture requires such attention to how education takes place, since it cannot fall back on unconscious processes and stable institutions to do its job. Furthermore, the history of education indicates that there is a definite trend toward institutional complexity, curricular diversity, and professionalization of the teaching force.

Types of Education in Our Culture

To meet the demands of the modern cultural situation, three types of education have emerged. Technical education is aimed at developing the useful life. Liberal education is directed toward the life of wisdom. Moral and religious education are concerned with the good life.

There has been considerable emphasis upon technical vocational education at the secondary level; for the most part technical and vocational schools provide what is known as terminal training in some particular calling. There is also increasing emphasis on professionalism at the level of higher education: teachers colleges, medical schools, engineering schools, and theological seminaries are examples of this trend. Technical education is education for the useful life through the inculcation of the necessary skills and knowledges.

Liberal education, on the other hand, stresses the great human riches, introducing the individual quite consciously to the tradition, culture, and civilization of which he is a part. The emphasis is upon his becoming not only an appreciative member of his culture but also a leader in and creator of that culture. With its concern for the languages and the classics, liberal education seeks to train the person to contribute to the life and thinking of his civilization. This is training for the life of wisdom.

In regard to moral and religious education, it must be remembered that a culture cannot remain stable and perpetuate itself without introducing each new generation to its standards, its cult, and its doctrine in a telling way. This is, of course, not necessarily Christian education. In fact, in our culture it is often not Christian education at all, since the cultural norms are secular and scientific. Education in morals, carried on in our public institutions of learning, has been demonstrated to be education in middle-class morality, not education in Christian ethics. Education in values, carried on in our public schools, is education in moral and spiritual values, and cannot become education in the Christian faith without breaking the law. Moral and religious education, taken in this sense, recognizes that a person can be competent in his field, can know and participate in the riches of his culture and civilization, and yet not be a person of complete dedication to the true, to the worthy, and to that which is of consummate value. Moral and religious education seeks to develop this dedicated life, transforming, as it were, the useful life and the life of wisdom into the life that is committed to the highest. The fact is that many educational groups (the National Education Association and the American Council on Education among them) and many educational philosophers and practitioners (from John Dewey on down) have worked seriously to discover how the schools may educate for commitment to high value. (See Ward Madden, *Religious Values in Education;* Harper & Brothers, 1951.)

RELIGIOUS EDUCATION AND CULTURE

This brief word about religious education in our culture needs to be seen against the background of the place that religious education has in various kinds of cultures.

Religion is an indispensable ingredient in maintaining and directing individual and social life. In every culture part of the learning that takes place in each new generation is religious learning. Religious education is undertaken by members of the culture in order to guide religious learning.

Religious education is society's way of introducing each new generation to the values that give its culture basic meaning. It is also society's way of bringing each new generation into direct and dynamic relationship with what it conceives as the power that controls its life. It consists of growth in participation in the cultic practices by which society maintains its relationship with the ultimate. It also consists in gradual apprehension of the doctrine by which society explains the meaning of life and history.

Whether religious education is formal or informal depends upon the same factor that determined the formality or informality of other educational processes: the degree to which cultural differentiation and conflict (and thus religious differentiation and conflict) are present.

In the hands of the priest, religious education tends to be culturally conservative in function, and relatively simple. In the hands of the prophet, it tends to be culturally reconstructive in function, and gains a simplicity from the sharpness of its purpose and motive. In the hands of the theologians, it tends to be apologetic and argumentatively dogmatic, conservative or reconstructive as the case may be, but increasingly complex in the institutions that it needs.

In a heterogeneous culture in which the religious question is not considered to be acute, the burden of religious education has to be carried by each communion, local church, and family. The heterogeneity of the culture intensifies the problem because the cultural core tends to exclude important aspects of religious experience and belief. Education in these aspects of experience and belief must be undertaken by what amount to religious segments of society.

Thus, even from a purely sociological standpoint, Protestant education, in most cases to be found only in places where it is in juxtaposition to other faiths, cannot count on the unplanned influences of the general culture to convey its tenets and practices to the next generation. It must do so itself in definitely planned and organized fashion. In its educational efforts it is swimming against the current, but without the urgency of a crisis to mobilize its efforts.

THE INDIVIDUAL, THE CULTURE, AND EDUCATION

The individual has been an important consideration throughout this discussion. Look at him now in another essential role. He is not always the docile recipient of the transmission of culture. He often needs to assert his integrity at the expense of the established culture. Sociology has studied and understands well the role of the reformer in culture; it is he who symbolizes frequently the breakdown of the old and the creation of the new.

How does it happen that such a powerful and enduring phenomenon as a culture can be thus at the mercy, it would seem, of a single man with a new idea? The reason provides one of the insights that is basic to education. There is only one way of transmitting a culture — each new generation must rediscover and re-create it for itself. In fact, each person in each new generation must rediscover and re-create it for himself. Education might even be defined as the process by which the individual in each new generation is helped systematically to remake the culture for himself. How much the reformer will be encouraged depends in part upon how much the culture obviously needs radical remaking, and in part on how strong and determined the custodians of the prevailing culture happen to be.

Some educators (Rousseau, for instance) have regarded

the culture as the enemy of the individual. This is an interesting possibility upon which to speculate, but seems to have limited validity.

The basic situation is clearly that the culture sustains its society (the individual, the family, the community, the nation), and in many informal ways is transmitted to each oncoming generation. As societies become more differentiated and subcultures develop, education takes on more formal and institutionalized aspects (schools come into existence, and special teaching orders appear in society).

The Rise of Educational Theory

It has been the increasing complexity of the educational task and the growth of the educational establishment that have occasioned the need for concentrated attention to educational theory. At the same time, the availability of scientific data on human nature, human development, personality, learning, and the functions of social groups and movements has provided a reservoir of ideas and possibilities constituting a science of education, to be channeled if and when we know our purposes and get our direction settled.

Part of the concern for educational theory has thus been a concern about the objectives of education. It is patently difficult for a complex and pluralistic culture to be clear about the objectives that should guide the operations of its educational establishment. The matter of objectives has, appropriately enough, been a matter of active negotiation among educators and citizens in America for over fifty years.

Educational theory must also give consideration to curriculum. Fundamentally, what shall be taught? How shall the content of education be selected from all the vast catalogue of our cultural experience? How shall the curriculum be designed as a dependable vehicle for guiding the learning that is desired and necessary? What teaching and learning methods shall be employed? This problem has been aggravated as the curriculum has sought to be more life-centered at the same time that the schools have come to center attention upon themselves as institutions. The curriculum has thus been forced to reproduce life situations in an artificial environment — an enterprise that even on the surface is not very promising.

Another part of the concern for educational theory has been with regard to administration. How shall the educational establishment itself be set up (organized)? How shall it be run (managed)? How shall it be inspected and improved (supervised)? How, in sum, shall educational institutions and the whole educational enterprise be made more fitting instrumentalities for the transmission and re-creation of culture?

These are pressing and vexing concerns, both for the educator and for the public — to say nothing of the student. The hope for education lies in the formation of theory that is thoroughly informed by the science of education, drawing as that science does upon the insights of the social sciences, philosophy, and history; and that consists of adequate objectives and dependable principles of curriculum and administration.

[3]

The Church
and Its Educational Problems

TODAY's cultural situation is bringing about radical alterations in our religious life. The culture is extremely heterogeneous, but may be said to be strongly secular and scientific. It tends to approach every aspect of life in a technical and specialized way. This culture is powerfully influencing the theology and life of the church.

The chief results of the pressures that the secular and scientific aspects of the culture have brought to bear upon the thought and life of the church are a technical and professionalized theology and a highly organized and promoted church life.

Christian education reflects the nature of the culture as it has affected both the church and education. Its aims have been stated in technical educational and theological terms. Its procedures have increasingly reflected the principles of the science of education. Its programs and institutions have been designed (or redesigned) in most cases by trained educators and theologians in professional terms.

Let no one casually shrug off the realism of this situation. It is all too close to us in every parish in the land. Actually, many of us have worked hard to bring it to pass by raising our standards, reorganizing our programs, replanning our curriculums, and retraining our workers.

But there is another aspect of this matter of the church

and its educational problems that appears to offer a serious challenge to this culturally produced situation in the church and its educational work. There is something about the church of Jesus Christ that deeply influences the way it educates. Christian education has a particular thrust. The very nature of the church prevents it from adopting uncritically any culture-bound educational system, or from substituting such a system for a process of education that grows out of and expresses what it really is as the church.

THE CHURCH AS A SOCIAL INSTITUTION

The hope of our nation, from a cultural point of view, is in reform, planning, and social engineering, using a scientific approach. The church as a social institution has not been exempt from this hope. Indeed, it has accepted it and used it gladly.

There can be no question but that the church is a social institution, and that as such it always tends to mirror its culture. The results of cultural conditioning on the life of the church are particularly evident today in its theology on the one hand, and in the way it does its work on the other.

Theology is the church's conscious explanation of its beliefs to itself and to the world. The theologian starts always with the premise that God has revealed himself to the human race. If the premise is that God has revealed himself through nature broadly conceived, or through some aspect of nature, theology becomes "natural theology," a position that is popular because it allows great latitude for a scientific approach to the matter. If the premise is that God has revealed himself in some way that transcends nature, theology becomes some form of supernaturalism. If the premise is that God has revealed himself in a special way in Jesus Christ and in the Scriptures, then theology becomes in some sense " Biblical theology." If the premise is that God has revealed himself in this special way, and also to the enlightened human mind, the result is " rational theology," or some form of scholasticism. The premises are many, and vary greatly, but the task of theology in relation to them is clear — it is the church's way of interpreting them to itself and to others.

The task of formulating Christian beliefs in terms that will make the Christian faith clear to any given generation is of course a recurring one. Christian beliefs need to be restated from time to time as the generations change, partly because of changes in language, but mostly because of what those changes in language signify, namely, a change in perspective or a change in the way people look at life. The job of theological reformulation is never finished because different cultures and changing ideologies constantly require that the church express its faith in different ways.

Let us be reminded that it is expected that a document like the Westminster Confession of Faith, which represents theology at its best, will need amendment from time to time. Provision is specifically made by the church for amending it. But there are no provisions for amending the Word of God, which is the Confession's premise. As a matter of fact, there are those who have given their lives to locating and eradicating unauthorized amendments which various ancient copyists have happened to insert in its text.

In this connection, it is interesting to reflect on the fact that the translating of the Bible into English will never be completed so long as English is a live language, and that every succeeding translation must be checked for accuracy

in two directions — first, with the original text, to be sure
that it is true to it; and secondly, with the culture of the
day as it is expressed in the language it uses, to be sure
that the meaning is communicated accurately in verbal
symbols that the culture can understand.

The church's theology in our day has been deeply influenced by several movements that have been instigated
by the culture. It has been the recipient of the results of
scientific Bible study, and has either adjusted to the methods and results of this discipline or become absorbed with
trying to rationalize its way out of accepting them. Theological formulations have had to be systematized in order
to meet the challenges of the rationalistic philosophies of
the day. And they have had to be unsystematized in order
to meet the challenges of the existentialist philosophies of
the day. It is also true that the church's theology has
yielded in some quarters to the blandishments of liberal
optimism. Nevertheless, it has sounded a much-needed
social note as the humanitarian movement has stabbed it
awake.

The difficulty has not been so much that theology has
made these adjustments, for in the main it had no alterna-
tive but to try to make them or to stop doing its job. The
difficulty has been, rather, that each change has had to be
explained to the church and the world so that the nature
of the adjustment, why it was made, and what its implications were would be clear. Thus reformulation has piled
on reformulation, debate on debate, and volume on volume, until the field of theology has become largely one
for specialists alone.

God has raised up these men to clarify the gospel for
our day, and they are trying to do so. But the uncertain
voice of the culture, and its basic alienation from the gos-

pel, makes their task of translation, interpretation, and communication extremely difficult.

Turning to the question of the influence of our culture on the church's life and work, we see that concentrated attention is being given by the church to a " program " that is highly organized and promoted. The church has become increasingly aware that in our cultural setting it cannot count on community or cultural atmosphere and influence to do its work for it. In the field of education, for instance, God has in our present era given the church a much more difficult task — that of helping to nurture the Christian life in a cultural setting that is in many ways hostile to it.

Vaguely mindful of this, the church has resorted in the last century to an increasingly institutionalized Christian education. Remembering that this represents only a segment of the church's program of worship, evangelism, mission, and the rest (and that all have been deeply affected by the same cultural factors), and that it does not by any means represent the one segment adequately, let us look at what many Protestant churches can boast by way of Christian education: a Sunday church school, several youth fellowships, a vacation church school, a weekday church school, communicants classes, adult study classes, Scout troops, missionary organizations for various ages, women's work, men's work, parents classes, adult study classes, church officer training programs, programs of religion in the home, and programs of leadership training. Some have parochial schools in addition. Beyond the local church is a denominational and interdenominational network of agencies for the promotion of various phases of Christian education.

Having to speak to a group of candidates for church vocations in Christian education not long ago, I quickly jotted down a list of the various types of full-time occupations in the field, so that I might indicate to them some of the possibilities. Hastily compiled, the list was very incomplete, but even so included twenty-one categories. All this speaks as a commentary on one phase of the church's existence as it seeks to do its work in this culture, and bears out the point that Christian education reflects the nature of the culture as it has affected both the church and education.

Perhaps the most serious aspect of the situation is revealed, however, in a proposition and a question on which I was asked to speak to a university class some years ago. The class had itself formulated them, and was quite happy over the fact that it had not forgotten to include the church in its syllabus. Here is what they presented to me: " The community produces the child and is responsible for him. What is the role of the church as part of the community in meeting his basic needs? "

THE CHRISTIAN CHURCH AND ITS EDUCATIONAL WORK

The church is a social institution, and as such always tends to reflect its culture. We have seen how this has happened in the church's theology and in its life and work in our day.

At the same time the church is the body of Christ, and as such tends to resist cultural inroads and to work for the redemption of culture. As Clarence Tucker Craig put it, " In the midst of human perplexity there is a community with Christ as its center, which is the promise and foretaste of a new society."

The church is the human instrumentality brought into being by God in Christ to continue his ministry of redemption to the world. It is the New Israel, sustained and guided in its work by the Holy Spirit. Its mission is universal, its mood and motive is love, and its education is nurture in the fellowship of love.

The church consists of Christ's disciples, his men and women, who seek to do his work in each generation. This helps to make clear what the church is and what it is not. The church is an organization, but only because it must have a social framework within which to work. It is a school, but only because the work of Christ involves constant instruction. It is a house of prayer, since God's church has always been instructed to assemble itself together before him. It is not just another community organization offering the means of pinning the badge of respectability on oneself. Nor are the church's responsibilities such that one may be absent from them at will.

Christian education is to be understood as part of the church's work in the world. The church, as the fellowship of the redeemed in Christ, together with their children, has many functions to perform, but among them are two that are directly educational in nature: the nurture of the young in the Christian faith and fellowship, and the systematic training of those outside its ranks who have heard the call of the gospel or are listening for it.

Experience has taught the church that systematic training, long-term nurture, and lifelong education are involved in fulfilling its mission. This is why the church has a teaching ministry — why Christian education is an essential part of its work.

Thus Christian education is the systematic and ordered nurture of the Christian life. Its aim is that each child, youth, and adult shall realize fully his discipleship.

THE CHURCH LOOKS AT THE CULTURE

Theology is the church's means of looking at its culture and weighing it. Difficult as this is to do, it can be done, and must be done by the church in each generation.

Christian theology cannot find much fault with the descriptions we have given of the roles of culture, education, religion, and religious education in the social process. Using the term " existential " in the Aristotelian sense, theology would consider what has been said an accurate delineation of the existential situation.

It is another story, however, when theology examines the status of culture. When uninformed by the Christian gospel, human culture becomes merely a way by which the race defends itself more or less blindly against the demands of the living God. Its cultural defense constitutes in that case a defiance, the eating of forbidden fruit, the erection of a golden calf, the building of altars to the gods of Canaan — the most radical form of sin. Any education, religion, or religious education that the culture devises and uses in this situation is not only a party to that sin, but succeeds in compounding it.

Christian theology does not call for the destruction of culture, however, any more than it calls for the destruction of the individual. In the case of the individual it asserts the need for repentance, new birth, and new life. In the case of the culture, theology asserts that a conversation is needed in which the church points the culture to the source of its strength — the living God and his Word, and to the direction it must take — the will of God for its people in the day and situation it serves.

Education, religion, and religious education under the gospel serve about the same functions as before, but with a completely different dynamic and orientation. The new dynamic is the Holy Spirit. The new orientation is the meaning of history and existence as seen in the gospel of God in Christ.

Richard Niebuhr, in his *Christ and Culture* (Harper & Brothers, 1951), has traced the history (primarily in intellectual terms) of what he calls " the double wrestle of the church with its Lord and with the cultural society in which it lives." He points out four options that Christians have held at various times in dealing with this problem: first, that the Christian faith and culture are antithetical (radical anticulturalism); secondly, that the Christian faith and culture can be accommodated to one another; thirdly, that the basic question is not that of the Christian faith and culture at all, but between a God who has made all things good and man who is in sin; and fourthly, that the Christian faith and culture are in a dynamic interpenetration with one another without the one ever really becoming the other or destroying the other. He concludes:

> " The problem of Christ and culture can and must come to an end only in the free decisions of individual believers and responsible communities. . . . To believe is to be united with both the One in whom we believe and with all those who believe in him. . . . The decisions are made . . . on the basis of relative insight and faith, but they are not relativistic. They are individual decisions, but not individualistic. They are made in freedom, but not in independence; they are made in the moment, but are not nonhistorical." (Used by permission.)

What is clearly implied is that the church must, in the dynamic tension of interpenetration of faith and culture, train people who are up to making such decisions. This is the logical outcome of the theological criticism of culture

—and points clearly to a difficult but urgent task for Christian education.

What Does the Christian Need by Way of Education?

We are now in a position to see education from the dual perspective of the culture and the church. The education of the individual is a shared process. It is shared by all the church's functions, none of which is without its educational implications. It is shared also by the institutions of education that are part of the secular culture. On the basis of such an understanding of the shared nature of education, we may ask what kind of education a Christian needs.

The Christian has many of the same educational needs that anyone else has. He has need for a technical education, that through the development and use of skills he may lead a useful life. He has need for a liberal education, that through knowledge and reflection he may lead a life of wisdom. He has need for a moral and religious education, that through discriminating choice and dedication to value he may lead a good life.

In connection with these three kinds of education, all of which minister to the Christian's needs, the aim of education might be put in this fashion: *that we may become persons who see things as they are and who come to grips with life*. This sounds simple, but is actually far-reaching. Later the question will be raised whether this aim can be achieved in a secular context, or whether it requires that the educational process find itself at a Christian level.

What further needs does the Christian have for education beyond the technical, the liberal, and the moral and religious? Look at who he is. The Christian is a man, a human being. We believe that he was created by the sov-

ereign God in his own image, but that being endowed with
the freedom to choose to be found within the reality and
will of God or to live by his own devices, he chose the
latter. He has willfully cut himself off from God, and
stands in need of reconciliation.

Only God can effect that reconciliation, but man accepts
or rejects it. Throughout history God spoke his reconciling
word many times, and engaged in many reconciling acts,
until finally, in a act of the most complete love for man,
God became human himself. He lived among men, teaching and healing them. Then, because sin cannot be rooted
out without the most intense suffering — suffering even
to the point of agonizing death — God put himself in
man's place; he suffered and died in agony instead of man.
God's love was so great, his sovereignty so complete, that
when it comes to a man's suffering and dying on account of
his rejection of him, he finds that this penalty for his crim-
inal situation has already been paid — by the very God
whom he has sinned against.

Then he rose from the dead. He lives.

Where does this leave man? Man has but to accept with
his whole heart what has been done on his behalf to be
free from pretense and to live in Christ by the indwelling
of the Holy Spirit. By faith in Christ as his Savior and his
Lord, he enters into fellowship with God. In the Christian
the gracious work of God for man is reflected in the personal act of faith.

This, then, is the need that technical, liberal, moral, and
religious education do not meet. These kinds of education
man must have because he is a man, a human being; but
without a Christian perspective they contain the seeds
of tragedy and despair. Without a Christian perspective
they are man's effort to live without God by his own

devices. What have they to say to a man's need for release
from the bondage of his human-centeredness? What have
they to say to his need for redemption? What have they to
say to his need for reconciliation to God?

But let me ask quite frankly the most decisive question
in the field of Christian education today: What has education to do at all with man's need for redemption and release from bondage through reconciliation? The current
rejection of the relevance of education by certain thinkers
is based upon the two facts that pose the dilemma: reconciliation is man's need and is God's act; education is a
human activity and would seemingly be able only to com-
pound man's involvement in sin.

Is *Christian* education, then, possible? Yes. Educational
activities have a legitimate place in leading a person to
know and accept what God has done for him. They have
a legitimate place in helping him to see things as they are
and to come to grips with life. They have a legitimate
place in helping a person to find and lead a life of fulfillment in Christ. There is no necessary contradiction between God's action and man's efforts. Education is not
necessarily and inevitably sin.

What is *distinctive* about Christian education? Christian
education ministers to the need for the redeemed life —
the life transformed by the God who created man in his
own image, revealed himself with redemptive clarity in
Jesus Christ, and guides ever by his Holy Spirit. The distinctive thing about Christian education is the ministry
of the Word, the Word that this God speaks.

Can all education be Christian, or must it remain partly
secular? Fundamentally all education can be Christian,
but only in the sense that the person approaches it as a
Christian. If he is in fellowship with God, a member of

the body of Christ, and bearing witness by word and life, then every educational effort will be received, interpreted, and used so that its effect is the furtherance of the Christian life. Thus technical, liberal, moral, and religious education may be transformed by the renewing power of the Holy Spirit, and may constitute part of the educational ministry to the Christian.

Reflect again for a moment: the aim of education is that we may become persons who see things as they are and who come to grips with life. Is this possible except from a fully Christian perspective?

Seeing things as they are implies realism — realism in viewing history and its meaning, realism in viewing the contemporary scene, realism in self-understanding. (These are so easy to say, yet so unbearable to the human spirit in many of their implications.) The realism of seeing things as they are means the recognition of God's sovereignty and judgment; the recognition of man's freedom, sin, responsibility, and need; the recognition of the significance of revelation and redemption; the recognition of and the incontrovertibility of hope. Seeing things as they are leads to clarity of idea and attitude, and to the clear motivation of completely realistic intention.

Coming to grips with life implies man's action within the context of things as they are, within the context of his culture. It means the acquisition of the personal and social skills needed for full and responsible participation in the work of the church and the world at every level. Full involvement in the work of the church and the world is required: membership, fellowship, discipleship, vocation, leadership, and mission.

Education with such aims inevitably implies a fully Christian perspective. To avoid a Christian perspective leads on the one hand to the substitution of secular religious values, whose fate is to stand outside the door of Biblical faith yearning for what lies within but unwilling to enter. Or it leads, on the other hand, to limitation of aim and even to bitterness and cynicism.

[4]

Past and Present
in Christian Education

THIS review of the cultural process, our present cultural situation, the role of education, and the church and its educational problems has established some findings that may help in understanding the way Christian education has developed in America, and that at the same time may assist in interpreting the present situation and devising an intelligent approach to it.

The present cultural situation in America is described as pluralistic (with no pervasive and encompassing common assumptions and values), dynamic (actively in search of unity of spirit), complex (given to compensating for its lack of cultural unity by highly organizing its various parts in order to maintain the fabric of society), secular (generally recognizing only human authority), and scientific (pinning its hopes on the findings of empirical investigation, and on planning and engineering based on them). The significance of this situation is driven home by a realization of the powerful and enduring character of this or any other culture in molding and guiding its members.

Education is described as the bridge between the culture and each new generation. While in a unified culture this process goes on in relatively informal ways, in our culture education has become an institutionalized science.

Our culture has developed three main kinds of education: technical education (whose aim is the useful life), liberal education (whose aim is the life of wisdom), and moral and religious education (whose aim is the good life, and whose norms are the culture's mores and values).

The individual remains a somewhat unpredictable factor, however, since he is not always content to be molded by his culture, but is relatively free to accept or reject its forms and influences. Nevertheless, education in our day has developed as an institutionalized science to the point where it is concerned with the building of its theoretical foundations, giving fitting place to the definition of its objectives, the delineation of its curriculum principles, and the setting up of its principles of administration.

The church in our day is engaged in finding itself in terms of the dilemma it has always faced, but which is particularly critical now — the dilemma that is posed by its being an institution inextricably bound up with its culture, and at the same time being the servant of its Lord. This dilemma becomes acute in the field of education, but it is suggested that the Christian need not settle for an education that is partly secular and partly Christian, for if education actually involves seeing things as they are and coming to grips with life, it can hardly be complete unless carried on within a fully Christian perspective.

The significance of these developments is easy to see in a review of the history of Christian education in America. Such a historical review will serve both to illustrate these trends and to set the stage for dealing with Christian education's outstanding present needs, which are the building of theory and the communication of theory.

The history of Christian education in America may be analyzed and understood best if it is dealt with in terms of three periods. The first period is one of beginnings, reaching back to the founding of Harvard, and coming to a close with the publication of Bushnell's *Christian Nurture* in 1846–1847. The second period is one of expansion and development, starting in the middle of the nineteenth century and ending with the great depression of 1929. The third period is one of consolidation and definition, having its roots back in the first quarter of the twentieth century and continuing through the present time.

THE BEGINNING PERIOD

The concern for Christian learning in the early days of the American colonies was manifest in the founding of institutions for the training of ministers. Harvard was the first of these, and similar institutions soon sprang up in other colonies. The interest in a trained ministry meant in those days that the communities concerned wanted to be certain that a properly educated person would be in their midst both to preach and to teach, for the position in many places was a combined one.

The first so-called "Sunday school" was founded in 1780 in Gloucester, England. It was a missionary and social welfare enterprise, inspired by the neglected condition of many of the children of the time. It met on Sunday because the children worked on other days, and its curriculum was a fairly broad one that included religion as one among several other subjects. Robert Raikes, the founder, was chiefly concerned to get the children off the streets and to provide them with the basic tools of learning. The Sunday school movement was indifferently received in some quarters, and was met with active hostility in others. However, this type of Sunday school was soon brought to America, and spread throughout the larger cities. In spite

of continued opposition to it, many leaders among both
clergy and laity supported the movement and participated
in it. Particularly significant is the fact that the Sunday
school was brought into existence as a result of Christian
concern over the breakdown of society in the early period
of the Industrial Revolution.

During the early part of the nineteenth century it became evident that the home, the church, and the general
community could not handle the educational problem
without the help of publicly supported and controlled
common schools. Various experiments were made along
this line, but the pattern for universal education in America was set by Massachusetts in the 1840's under the guidance of Horace Mann. Mann had studied educational systems in Europe, and in a series of annual reports during
that decade mapped out the plans for public education
that have found almost universal acceptance throughout
the United States. Most important for our purposes was
his recommendation that the schools be separated from
any church control, that anything of a sectarian nature
be excluded from the curriculum, and that the schools
limit themselves in the realm of religious education to the
serious moral development of their pupils. This solution
to the problem of the sectarian aspects of education was
prompted by local difficulties between various Protestant
groups. It was not Mann's intention to exclude the Bible
from the schools or to neglect the inculcation of Christian
morality. But as the society that the common school served
became infinitely more heterogeneous than it was at that
time, his general policy was applied in such a way that it
has resulted in the exclusion from the schools of elements
of religious education that he took for granted as part of
the school's responsibility. Thus Christian education has in

fact become in most cases the exclusive responsibility of the home and the church.

The fundamental situation that Christian education had to face was fast taking shape during these years toward the middle of the nineteenth century. It was just at this time that Horace Bushnell wrote his *Christian Nurture,* in which he expressed views that are now considered to be the basis for the modern development of religious education. Bushnell was outraged by the neglect on the part of so-called Christian families of the Christian education and nurture of their children, and also by the tendency of the revivalism of the day to play sensationally on the theme of the separation of children from God until the time of their conversion. Although he was criticized for the unorthodoxy of certain of his views, there can be no doubt of his adherence to the belief in the covenant relationship between God and the Christian family. Thus he propounded and defended the thesis that " they [children in the Christian family] are to grow up Christian and never know themselves to be otherwise." He based this thesis upon the text that states that the responsibility of Christian parents to their children is to " bring them up in the nurture and admonition of the Lord " (Eph. 6:4). The result of the publication of these views was mainly to stir a small flurry of theological controversy. Then interest in the matter died down. Bushnell himself did not bother to follow it up, except to expand his book and answer his first critics. The influence of his views did not begin to be felt until the turn of the century, but has been steadily gaining since then, so that he is now considered to be the leading figure in Christian education theory in the nineteenth century, and the precursor of our present work in the field of Christian education.

THE PERIOD OF EXPANSION AND DEVELOPMENT

The rise of the common school, with its exclusion of sectarian education, left the task of Christian education up to the home and the church. Neither rose to the occasion. Concerned Christian laymen, however, casting about for a solution to the problem, found in the Sunday school a vehicle that could be readily adapted to the developing need. So the movement that had begun as a missionary and social welfare effort was adapted to become the medium for specifically Christian education. It remained a lay movement, but its curriculum was narrowed down to religious instruction alone, and its schedule (it had been at the beginning an all-day school) was greatly curtailed. The result was that the Sunday school practically as we now know it was born.

The Sunday school movement during this period was distinguished by its efforts in leadership development, curriculum development, and the development of supplementary services.

In leadership development, the outstanding early events were a series of conventions for the training and inspiring of Sunday school leaders, most of whom were volunteers. Begun in 1832, these conventions exerted more and more influence, until in 1872 it was recognized that they were the controlling factor in the movement. It was not until 1899, however, that the idea of a permanent staff took hold, indicating the consistently lay and volunteer character of the movement up to that time. Sunday school associations, manned by laymen, reaching into practically every community in the country, and organized in a pyramid of county and state associations, ran the movement, which remained largely outside the organization and control of the denominations. Practically nothing remains of this movement at the present time, the work having been taken over almost entirely by the denominations and their allied interdenominational agencies. The conventions are still held, and are well attended, but they are planned and run in the main by the executive staffs of the denominational boards and by staff people from the Division of Christian Education of the National Council of Churches. Even though they continue, many denominational executives seriously question their worth as leadership training enterprises.

Lay leaders of the Sunday school movement also pioneered in setting up summer schools and conferences for leadership training, a singularly successful type of work. This aspect of leadership development has also been largely taken over by the denominations, and continues to be operated on an ever-expanding scale.

In curriculum development, the National Sunday School Convention in 1872 succeeded in bringing order out of chaos by adopting the Uniform Lesson system. These lessons were based on Biblical content, served pupils of all ages, were outlined by an interdenominational committee, and alternated in a six-year cycle between the Old and the New Testaments. It is noteworthy that in order to arrive at an organizing principle on which all could agree, Biblical content was chosen. Organizing principles that had to be rejected were Christian doctrine, churchmanship, the church year, the Christian life, and others. One of the most difficult tasks in curriculum development in our present period has been to break away from this narrowly conceived Biblical basis for the curriculum, and to develop a more inclusive foundation for it. The most important later developments in curriculum during the period of

expansion were in the direction of grading — the introduction of various types of graded lessons, particularly the
closely graded lessons (where a different lesson is provided
each Sunday for each grade) and the group graded lessons,
sometimes called departmental or cycle graded lessons
(where a different lesson is provided for each department,
operating usually on a three-year cycle).

In the development of supplementary services, three
types of service were particularly important. In order to
reach children outside the church, the vacation was hit
upon as an ideal time for Christian education, and the
vacation school came into existence. With the same motivation, arrangements were arrived at with many public-
school systems whereby one hour per week could be given
to religious instruction, and the weekday church school
was born. A more concentrated form of educational service, usually including the Sunday school, the vacation
school, the weekday school, and many other activities, was
developed in church settlement houses. All these supplementary services were originally missionary in character,
but all are now well-recognized aspects of the work of most
Protestant churches, with the result that the Sunday school
movement has expanded to include many more aspects of
the pupil's Christian education than was the case at the
beginning.

The period of expansion and development saw not only
the rise of the modern Sunday school, the inclusion of
many types of service in its program, and its extension
beyond a program limited to Sunday — it also saw the
start and the growth of a large and vigorous youth movement.

The first major evidence of the need for a youth movement came with George Williams' founding of the Young

Men's Christian Association, in 1844, in England. The movement came to the United States in 1851, and has since become firmly rooted here, international in scope, and the pattern for other youth organizations. Again, this was a lay movement, and has remained so, with no organic connection with the church.

The Young People's Society of Christian Endeavor was founded in Maine in 1881, and soon spread to become national and international. Its motto was " For Christ and the Church," and although it again had no organic connection with the church, its groups met for the most part in churches, for purposes of religious and spiritual enrichment. The society developed a vast organization that paralleled the church, but it was never under church control. For this reason, since the assertion by the churches of control over their programs of Christian education, it has been pushed aside by many communions.

Thus the organization and program of Christian education during this period was largely developed and controlled by lay people, working outside the organic structure of the church. The need for such organization and program was obvious from the speed with which it was taken up and the proportions to which it grew. The need was reflected in a zeal and enthusiasm on the part of volunteers who organized, promoted, and led it.

Late in this period (toward the turn of the century) men in the general field of education became interested in the possibilities in religious education. There was at the same time a group of young professors and research men in the field of psychology of religion and religious education who were beginning to take a professional interest in the field. Representatives of these two groups were instrumental in founding the Religious Education

Association in 1903. The association, which is still in vigorous existence, had an interfaith membership, which was possible since all members joined strictly as individuals, and since the association was limited in function to providing a forum for discussion of problems and issues. Furthermore, its membership came from both education and religious education, giving it the opportunity to fulfill its purpose of "interpreting education to religion and interpreting religion to education." In this association what is usually referred to as the religious education movement found a voice. The influence of the movement on church schools has been chiefly to help them to become responsibly educational. Its influence on the public schools has been chiefly in the area of the development of character education.

At the same time as the Sunday school movement, the youth movement, and the religious education movement were taking hold, the field of higher education was also being developed. It was during this period that the greatest number of church-related colleges were being founded. Although state-sponsored higher education was not far behind, and was generally to move ahead of them, the church-related colleges and universities rendered the greater service for the times.

THE PERIOD OF CONSOLIDATION AND REDEFINITION

The present period in Christian education is one of consolidation and redefinition. The consolidation in the field has been in the nature of a closer co-ordination and integration of effort. The redefinition has been in relation to theological understandings and educational theory. In *The Task of Christian Education* (Chapter 1), I indicated that the 1920's, up to the depression of 1929, was a period of creative development, followed by about fifteen years of curtailment and criticism (the curtailment due to the depression and World War II, and the criticism due to the revival of theological interest), this period of curtailment and criticism being followed in turn by one of restudy. Currently there is a revival of interest and participation in Christian education throughout the United States.

The period of consolidation and redefinition can best be understood in terms of three influences: the educational, the denominational, and theological.

The educational influence was paramount in the early years of the period. The major concern of Christian education was with gaining educational validity through curriculum development and the perfecting of the educational plant. George Albert Coe, of Union Theological Seminary and Teachers College in New York City, was the acknowledged leader. His books *A Social Theory of Religious Education* (1917) and *What Is Christian Education?* (1929) were widely read and followed.

The educational influence has not diminished, although it was first challenged and then joined by the theological influence. There is just as keen concern for all the technical problems of an educational nature as ever before. In the church schools the concern is for the definition and use of objectives, for thoroughgoing curriculum development, for the enrichment and refinement of methodology, and for all phases of educational administration, particularly supervision. In the public schools the concern is for the proper understanding and use of moral and spiritual values, and for experimentation with teaching about religion (as contrasted with the teaching of religion) at various appropriate points in the curriculum.

The denominational influence of the period has already

been alluded to. By the early part of the twentieth century it began to be obvious to the denominations that the independent movements (the Sunday school and youth movements in particular) would have to be brought under church control. The formation of the International Council of Religious Education, in 1922, climaxed a long struggle to accomplish this control. The International Council primarily represented the executive staffs of the denominational boards of education, and took over the work that had previously been the province of both the denominations and the independent movements. One of the symbols of this important change was the alteration of the popular nomenclature, in which the " Sunday " school became the " church " school.

In the 1940's denominational control over the youth movement became almost universal. The organization of denominational " fellowships " became the rule, these fellowships co-operating together in the United Christian Youth Movement (connected with the International Council of Religious Education) . This did not materially affect the Y.M.C.A. or the Y.W.C.A., since they and the various Scout organizations co-operated in the new movement, but it did seriously curtail the openness with which the churches were likely to welcome other independent movements.

A further step toward the consolidation of the work was taken when the National Council of Churches was founded. The International Council and the Christian education interests of several ecumenical organizations were then brought into even closer working relationship. The strengthening of the ecumenical principle guaranteed that this new organization could never operate independently of the denominations that made it up, but could in fact only work at their behest. Thus the denominational influence on the Christian movement was deeply felt.

The same denominational influence was felt in the field of higher education. Practically every denomination increased its financial responsibility for the colleges with which it was connected, and strengthened its supervisory relation to them. There has been a conscious attempt on the part of the colleges to develop a basis for their work that expresses a deep-seated Christian philosophy of higher education. Nels F. S. Ferré, after consultation with the National Council of Churches, wrote his *Christian Faith and Higher Education* to help meet this need (Harper & Brothers, 1954). The Jamestown College (North Dakota) conference gathered an illustrious group to deal with this problem. Their contributions have been published in *Toward a Christian Philosophy of Higher Education* (John Paul von Grueningen, editor; The Westminster Press, 1957).

The theological influence on Christian education began to be felt during the 1930's. The Continental theologians (Barth and Brunner, in particular) were beginning then to be known and studied in the United States. Although there had been criticism at various times of the theological tenor of the Christian education work being done (Wilfred Evans Powell's book, *Education for Life with God;* Abingdon Press, 1934, is a good example of the most responsible criticism of this type), no serious theological challenge had been offered. With the publication of H. Shelton Smith's diatribe (*Faith and Nurture;* Charles Scribner's Sons, 1941), it was clear that the challenge had been offered and could not be ignored. The Study of Christian Education (summarized by Paul H. Vieth in *The Church and Christian Education;* The Bethany Press,

1947) was devoted largely to this matter. Much of the most creative work in Christian education has been at the point of discovering how to deal with theological issues in the construction of Christian education theory (men like James D. Smart, Lewis Joseph Sherrill, and Randolph Crump Miller have helped here) , and at the point of curriculum revision in view of the demand for theological validity (for instance, in the Presbyterian *Christian Faith and Life:* A Program for Church and Home, and the Protestant Episcopal Seabury Series) .

AN ESTIMATE OF THE PRESENT SITUATION

This review of the historical development of Christian education in America indicates something of how we have arrived at the present situation. We are now faced with the expectation of an even more highly organized and professionalized Christian education program than before, and with the difficulties involved in achieving theological validity for the program.

It may help us to decide on suitable action to be taken on the problem if we take stock of what appear to be our present commitments. They are theological, educational, and denominational.

Our theological commitments in Christian education at the present time are to a position that is supernaturalistic, Biblical, Christocentric, and ethical. There are strong tendencies also toward commitment to a higher doctrine of church than before, and to some rather specific eschatological views. It is fairly generally conceded that the objectives of Christian education must be in keeping with these theological commitments, as well as with our educational ideas.

Our educational commitments appear to be somewhat

as follows: to a conception of education that recognizes that it takes place throughout the life span; to a broad idea of the locus of education as including the church, home, community, and the individual himself; to an " inclusive and well-rounded " approach; to technical proficiency in curricular, methodological, and administrative matters; but still to volunteer leadership at the teaching level, with a combination of volunteer and professional leadership at the administrative level.

Our denominational commitments are to a strong organization and program that are predominantly denominational in character, with certain specific areas of responsibility assigned by the denominations to interdenominational agencies which they themselves set up and control.

In terms of the situation we are dealing with, and with respect to commitments like these, two outstanding needs emerge — the need for the building of theory by which these commitments may be both checked and implemented, and the need for the communication of theory to those who are doing various aspects of the job.

The building of theory will consist of spelling out the implications of theology and the science of education in terms that can be used by the church in its educational work.

The communication of theory is a matter of making the objectives, curriculum, and administration of Christian education clear to those who are responsible for planning the program, to those who are responsible for administering it, to those who teach and lead, and to those who are the learners.

After showing how the theory of Christian education may be built, we will turn to the matter of the communication of theory. As we deal with the communication of theory we will be able to see how an adequate theory may be expressed to those who plan, administer, teach, lead, and learn. With this understanding, we can return to the question of what the theory of Christian education should be and proceed to the building of a theory that can be communicated to and used by all who are involved.

[5]

Building a Theory
of Christian Education

IF IT IS to fulfill the demands that are now being made upon it (to say nothing of future demands), Christian education needs to get a new sense of direction and a new conception of its job. It cannot be content to tinker with curriculum, methods, and administrative arrangements. Christian education must see itself afresh in the light of the church's faith, life, and work, and in terms of the needs of the world and the persons it serves. In other words, a deep self-understanding is needed, a theory that undergirds its existence and informs everything that is done.

The modern cultural situation has forced the consideration of theory upon leaders in other types of education, and is beginning to make the same impact upon Christian education. The things we do as educators become less and less effective as time goes on if they are the result of selection by mere happenstance, with no thoroughgoing rationale for their use. The same is the case with Christian education.

Does this place the practical man over against the man of theory? Not at all. Rather, it discriminates between their functions and makes clear that what we need in times like ours are clear-eyed and knowledgeable theorists and practical men who will undertake to conduct the practical affairs of Christian education in the light of the best in theory available.

James McBride Dabbs, writing on the subject of race relations in the South, drew this distinction in a way that applies equally well to Christian education:

> "What are practical men? They are the men who, given the end, figure out the means. They know how to . . . attain a desired result. . . . The practical men did not, as practical men, create these desires; but, given the desires, they go to work. . . .
>
> "When the desires of a community become confused and conflict with one another, when accepted ends begin to grow either undesirable or impracticable, or both, then the typical practical man, who is a master of means, is most at sea. What is needed is a theorist in the root meaning of that word: a man who can see the whole picture and clarify for the community its conflicting desires. When the community again decides what it wants, the practical man is called in to obtain it." (*The Christian Century*, September 19, 1956. Copyright, 1956, Christian Century Foundation. Reprinted by permission.)

The construction and use of theory in Christian education involves the foundation disciplines and Christian education's operational aspects, with theory acting as the connecting link between them. The foundation disciplines are to be known and mastered so that Christian educators may be aware of what the basic issues and resources are. Furthermore, the foundation disciplines are to be known and mastered in as thorough, comprehensive, and systematic a way as possible. Thus integrity will not give way to superficiality, and premature concern for the "application of scientific (or other) findings" will be avoided. The operational aspects of Christian education are also to be made relevant so that Christian educators may be fully aware of the problems and responsibilities they face, and so that they may become competent in the practice of their craft.

Theory consists of working hypotheses, or principles (principles are dependable guides to practice), and in Christian education the working hypotheses upon which we base our work must be grounded in and derived from the foundation disciplines, while at the same time offering practical and pointed guidance for the operations that are conducted. Thus they constitute a body of principles that guide Christian education in the areas of objectives, curriculum, and administration. That body of principles is constantly subjected to revision, however, because of changes in the findings of the disciplines upon which it is founded, changes in the needs of Christian education as it is practiced, and changes that are the result of success or failure of the principles as they are subjected to operational testing.

The development and improvement of the theory of Christian education, then, depends upon the elaboration of its working hypotheses, or principles, and their constant refinement as the result of further research, both disciplinary and practical.

THE FOUNDATIONS FOR THEORY

Sound theory demands the mastery and application of certain concepts drawn from the field of theology, the church's life and work, philosophy and the philosophy of education, history and the history of education, psychology and educational psychology, sociology and educational sociology, and the new field of communications. Our question in each case is, What necessary contribution does this discipline make to a theory of education that is fundamentally Christian?

In *The Task of Christian Education* (Chapter 3), I showed how these foundation disciplines are used to inform the principles of Christian education. They provide clues to many of the pertinent questions that must be raised as a basis for such theory, as well as providing useful answers to these questions. Theology provides the normative Christian understanding of God, man, sin, redemption, history, society, responsibility, and destiny. The church's life and work provide the basis for seeing education as a function of the community of faith in its various aspects. Philosophy gives help in dealing with questions of reality, knowledge, and value from the point of view of man's quest; philosophy of education provides the particular educational perspective on these matters. History gives insight into trends that may affect the present situation and the future; history of education centers on educational trends and influences. Psychology penetrates the status and meaning of the human mind, body, and behavior; educational psychology applies these findings to specifically educational questions, thus enabling us to discover the first principles of learning, motivation, and the like. Sociology delves into the nature and operations of social groups and movements; educational sociology sees these findings in the light of the problems of the school, the whole educational enterprise, and society. Stemming from psychology and sociology alike, the new discipline of communications explores the ways in which ideas and attitudes are transmitted and appropriated from one person, group, and culture to another.

It is from these foundations that the two major concerns of Christian education theory — theology and the science of education — stem. In a way, they sum up the disciplines in terms of their most significant present impact on the field of Christian education.

How Christian Education Has Reacted to the Foundation Disciplines

Christian education has had to take account of both the developing science of education and the rise of theological concern in our day.

It has responded to the development of the science of education in several ways, not in any one consistent fashion. Sometimes it has accepted its ways uncritically. On occasion it has in amateur fashion tried to supplement the work of general education, using fragments of educational insights to guide it. In some cases it has selected what it could use from the science of education with critical discrimination. Rarely, it has pioneered where the science of education has followed.

Its response to the rise of theological concern has been one of the most interesting developments of our times. At first stubbornly resistant to the inroads of theology, and still reluctantly in some quarters, it has allowed itself to be guided by theology's insights into Christian truth. It has begun to embody these insights in its curriculum. This has forced it to reconsider the matter of objectives. It is only beginning to become aware that the insights of theology are also applicable to the administrative matters with which it is concerned.

The response to theology has varied from communion to communion, with some remaining antitheological, some seriously trying to be theological, and others trying various combinations of theological insights and insights from other sources. My own position is that Christian education can and must be theologically thorough and accurate, and at the same time maintain educational integrity and soundness.

THEORY AND PRACTICE

The content of theory consists of the objectives of the educational process, its curriculum principles, and its principles of administration. If these are derived from and checked against the best that is available from all the foundation disciplines, from theology through communications, then they will provide the theologically accurate and educationally sound base that is needed for the development of educational programs and operations.

By " objectives " is meant the purposes, goals, aims, and intentions of Christian education. By " curriculum " is meant all the procedures that Christian education utilizes, including content, methods, and materials. By " administration " is meant the whole process of planning, organizing, managing, and supervising the educational programs and institutions that are involved.

The objectives of Christian education are used to guide the planning of the curriculum, the application of curriculum principles to the work of Christian education being checked at every point in terms of its purposes. The shape, pattern, and structure of the curriculum are the determining factors in devising administration, the application of the principles of administration thus being made in terms of the demands of the curriculum. From both curriculum and administration, in operation, results are forthcoming. These may be evaluated by checking them against the objectives that are being sought.

The tragedy of practice without theory is that it has operated in the little triangle of curriculum, administration, and results. But no questions were raised about why particular educational procedures were being used, why the setup was handled in this particular way, or whether

the results forthcoming were adequate and valid. Practice
without theory is thus divorced from its sources, and has
no way of enriching, changing, and reconstructing itself
except by mere whim or fancy. Furthermore, it has little
or no intelligent reference to objectives, either at the point
of guiding the process or at the point of evaluating its results.

This is why I feel so keenly that in a day when the culture presents such a definite and cutting challenge to the
Christian faith, when the temper of the times is contrary
to the Christian understanding of God, man, society, and
destiny, Christian education practice uninformed by thoroughgoing theory represents a desperate failure in Christian stewardship.

Consistent Christian education practice must thus be
based upon an informed and responsible theory. That
theory has yet to be spelled out, but it may be seen that
it calls at least for the mastery of the practical arts of planning, organization, management, and supervision; method
of teaching; the organization of learning experiences into a
comprehensive and graded curriculum; the discriminating
use of the various agencies of Christian education; the
training of competent leaders; and the grasp of the various
personal roles that involve leadership in the whole process
of nurture and training.

How the Foundations Are Used in Building Theory

It has been hard not to give the impression that there
are little nuggets of educational wisdom glistening forth
from theology and the other foundation disciplines, simply
waiting to be gathered into a theory of Christian education. In a way, the foundation disciplines are directly use-

ful in the formulation of Christian education theory, since they do deal with the basic concerns of education and define the various aspects of the field of human and divine relationships that are of educational concern. But when we say that educational principles are to be derived from these disciplines, we are really saying that we must propound educational questions to them, expecting to receive from them answers that in many cases will be in their terms alone, sometimes contradictory from one discipline to another, and badly in need of translation and mutual reconciliation to be of any use to education. Only a beginning has been made at this, in the disciplines of the philosophy of education (where educational questions are put to philosophy), history, psychology, and sociology (which likewise have begun to be probed for educational guidance).

There is no " theology of education " in this sense. There is no " Christian philosophy of education " as yet, nor any other specifically Christian disciplinary analysis. It is the task of Christian education theory over the years to work at this matter.

The same procedures, however, may be used in the formulation of Christian education theory that have been used in deriving the educational implications of the various disciplines. The questions to which Christian education needs answers may be put to these disciplines.

We know what these questions are, and are thus in a position to ask the questions, even if our knowledge has not gone deep enough to enable us to receive very good answers as yet.

In order to get at the matter of objectives there are three questions to which we need answers: What categories of objectives are called for? What shall the objectives be in each of these categories? How shall the objectives be employed?

In order to get the curriculum principles we need, there are ten questions to which we must have answers: (1) What are the curriculum's distinctive contributions to the accomplishment of the task of Christian education? (2) Are such principles as comprehensiveness, balance, sequence, and flexibility valid for curriculum building? (3) What elements are to be included in the curriculum? (4) What organizing principle shall be used to guarantee the curriculum's unity? (5) How shall objectives be used in the curriculum? (6) How shall the curriculum be designed? (7) How shall curriculum materials be built? (8) Who shall be responsible for curriculum building? (9) How shall the curriculum be evaluated, and by what criteria? (10) How shall proper use of curriculum materials be guaranteed?

In order to get the principles of administration we need, there are three questions to which we must have answers: How and by whom shall the program be planned and organized? How and by whom shall the program be managed? How and by whom shall the program be supervised, that is, standardized, evaluated, and systematically improved?

This, then, is how the theory of Christian education is to to be built. This is how dependable operating principles (guides to practice) are to be derived. It will be our task when we deal with educational objectives, educational procedures, and educational programs and institutions later on (in Chapters 8–10) to give answers to these questions.

There is, however, another matter that must be considered before we do that. A theory could very easily be spelled out that would, to be blunt, speak to no one. In its very form as well as its substance, a theory of Christian education must take account of the people for whom it is built — the volunteer administrator, the untrained teacher and leader, and the pupil himself. They must be able to hear, comprehend, and use it. This calls for attention to the matter of the communication of theory.

[6]

The Communication
of Theory

IF OURS were a Christian culture, Christian assumptions about the meaning of life and existence and a Christian way of life would provide the essential unity. Christian education in such a setting would take place mainly through growth in participation in the family, church, and community, and the adoption, under the guidance of the Holy Spirit, of their beliefs and practices. Such educational institutions as existed would be largely incidental to this major thrust of informal education.

We have seen, however, that in our secular and scientific culture Christian education has become highly institutionalized. Both home and community have turned over responsibility for Christian training to the church and at the same time have expected from the church a professional level of operation in the educational work that it has to carry on.

But the fact is that the development of the church's educational institutions has been largely in the hands of relatively untrained lay people. It is only lately that the church as such has shown even any real inclination to take hold of Christian education, control it, and assume the responsibilities involved in its control.

God has put at the church's disposal in our day all the technical knowledge that the sciences of man have uncovered, with the result that Christian education may take full advantage of the emerging science of education and the experiences that secular groups have had with the institutional aspects of education. We have seen how this may be accomplished in the construction of Christian education theory.

God has also raised up a generation of leaders in the church who have rediscovered and restated the gospel for our time. But this has again been done largely in technical ways, understandable only to the professionally trained theologian. We have seen how these findings, technical as they are likely to be, may be used in building the basis for Christian education.

The purposes of Christian education, and its principles of curriculum and administration, have been formulated and are being formulated mainly in the light of technical educational theory and technical theology. Thus the emergence of the science of education, an institutionalized education, and the theological exposition of the Christian faith have been and are being brought into focus for the use of Christian education.

The Untrained Layman

But the untrained layman who does much of the running of and the teaching in our churches is not skilled in the science of education or in technical theological matters. He has been far more profoundly influenced by society's understanding of the meaning, aims, and goals of existence than he realizes, for he has been nourished from infancy in the cultural matrix that gave him birth. The rediscovery and restatement of the gospel for our times has also been " over his head," for it has been done by the professionally trained theologian largely in technical terms.

The managing and teaching layman has usually done the best he could with what he had, and in many cases he has done exceedingly well. But neither his theological understanding nor his educational background and skill have been adequate to the task that he has been given.

Thus, Christian education practices and institutions that have been constructed and run by laymen in terms they could understand and were at home with could be, and in most cases have been, a far cry from the proposals that have been made for Christian education in terms of an adequate theology and a sound educational practice. The dilemma (stated in greatly oversimplified terms) might be said to be that of the theologian and professional educator versus the volunteer.

The fact is that Christian education today is trying to do a professional job with inadequate personnel, institutions, and materials. Our present best efforts in Christian education can only be understood as attempts to adapt what we think should be to the limitations of the personnel and the situation within which we must work.

We need, therefore, in order to overcome this difficulty in a statesmanlike way, to state and express the theory of our work in a fashion that the untrained person may grasp. This not only will be of service to the layman; in all probability it will be of value to everyone, professional or lay, who plans, administers, teaches, leads, and learns, since it will provide a healthy and readily comprehensible basis for the common understanding of Christian education by all.

How Various Groups Have Handled the Problem

The Roman Catholics avoid the problem of the specialist versus the volunteer by taking all education into their own hands, providing their own trained teaching orders, and conducting the educational enterprise on a rather highly technical educational and theological level.

Public education is geared to adjusting the individual to the secular scientific world, and thus avoids the problem of theological foundations. Its procedures are technically educational, carried on in the light of the science of education. It eschews theology, except where it appears in a palatable form like " the public philosophy," " the traditions of civility," or " moral and spiritual values."

Jewish education holds to the policy of supplementary education (like Protestantism), but conducts it on a scale considerably expanded beyond the Protestant pattern, and with professional leadership.

Protestant education has, in the main, held that it could handle its educational needs through support of the public school (holding that the public school's purposes were basically Protestant). It has thus taken advantage of a large segment of education conducted in the context of the science of education. To accomplish the distinctive tasks of Protestant nurture it has provided various kinds of supplementary education. At the same time it has been content with untrained volunteer leadership in this area. This espousal of the policy of supplementary education, together with its largely uncritical dependence on the public school, has led to the problem we are discussing, and the need for Protestant education to clarify its views.

THE NEED FOR A GUIDING PRINCIPLE

The church's present problem in Christian education is that of discovering how to use to the greater glory of God the new knowledge in education and theology that is available to it, in spite of the fact that its educational practitioners are largely lacking in professional training in either field, and in spite of the fact that its existing institutions operate at a level that is for the most part far below a professional standard.

The problem is one of constructing a theory of Christian education that may be readily communicated to the people who will have to do the work at every level. They will have to be able to grasp the Christian faith adequately, and also take hold of the skills and understanding of how learning takes place and how personality develops.

The construction of a theory of Christian education that may be communicated readily is not quite so simple even as the analysis that we made of the building of theory would indicate. The answer is not so much in the elaboration of principles for Christian education (which is theory's task and which may be done without too much concern for getting its results across) as in the pointing up of those principles to the place where a clear guiding principle emerges — one that will make the particular thrust of Christian education evident, completely evident, to the practitioner in the field.

The difference between a guiding principle for Christian education and the other principles that constitute Christian education theory is that the guiding principle would suggest, infuse, and steer the whole matter: it would be at the heart of the setting of objectives; it would guide and check every procedure and method employed in the curriculum; it would serve as a guide to the selection of curriculum content; it would suggest how Christian education should be set up, run, and improved; it would serve as a guide to pruning out any administrative system and device that was not really germane to the church's faith, life, and work.

If there could be one such guiding principle, then what Lewis Mumford hopes for in higher education would be achieved in Christian education. What he suggests (in *Values for Survival;* Harcourt, Brace and Company, Inc., 1946) is that higher education needs one great idea to guide it; such an idea would act like a magnet, instantly polarizing the whole field. A magnet, he reminds us, can polarize a field of iron filings in a split second, accomplishing thereby more than could be done by an infinitely long process of patient, antlike construction.

The proper guiding principle could act as a magnet in Christian education, polarizing the whole field of human, natural, and divine relationships in terms of the very heart of the Christian message.

The guiding principle for Christian education must be a genuine principle, a dependable guide to practice. It must be the focus for other principles. It may under these conditions become the means by which educational and theological insights become translated into practice.

CRITERIA FOR THE GUIDING PRINCIPLE

The guiding principle for Christian education, if it is to be genuinely the focus for theory, and at the same time communicable to all, must be adequate, simple, and clear.

It must be theologically adequate. It must thus be theologically central and convincing. It must be able to stand up under the most searching theological criticism.

It must be educationally adequate. It must be informed by, and its implications developed in terms of, the educational disciplines.

In terms of all that has been said it is clear that Christian education will get its guiding principle from " education in the light of theology " — or, to put it more accurately, Christian education will be the education of man in the light of God.

The guiding principle must be integral to the elements that make up Christian education, unifying and focusing them. Thus it must be the very heart of the process of coming to grips with the Christian faith through the Bible, through Christian history, through doctrine, through the understanding of the physical world, through the life of society, through the life of the culture, through dealing with the various kinds of opposition to the Christian faith, through developing the various aspects of practical church-manship, and through engaging in the Christian mission. At the same time it must be at the very heart of the process of growing in the Christian life through self-under-standing, through understanding and dealing with the fact of sin, through the experience of redemption, through worship, through prayer, through meditation, through being a member of the church, through working in and through the church, and through ethical and responsible living in the family, the community, the school, and else-where.

It must be simple, in the sense that it may be compre-hended in a single proposition, or a brief series of closely related propositions.

It must be clear in that it must be readily, easily, and unmistakably understandable.

These criteria, if observed, might be of telling assistance in identifying the needed guiding principle for Christian education, since if such a principle is adequate, it will meet the requirements of education and theology, and if it is simple and clear, it will meet the needs of those Christian educators who lack professional training in education and theology.

Here, then, is a clue worth following in the search for a theory of Christian education that is genuine and at the same time communicable.

Some Possible Alternatives

In the light of these criteria, examine some of the suggestions that have been made seriously from time to time for Christian education's guiding principle. With the exception of one, each of the focuses for Christian education to be considered has been suggested by some individual or group in the field as the appropriate center of attention.

In each case its proponents have said that if Christian education would focus its attention on this element, it would do its job as it should be done. They have insisted that around this element the other elements may be grouped, but that this is the one that can stand alone and give the others meaning. This is the essential element in setting up Christian education and devising its curriculum.

Some suggest that the Bible be the center of Christian education. Logically, doctrine could also be considered a possible center, although no one actively supports the idea. The proponents of this principle most often mean the transmission of knowledge of the content of the Bible or doctrine. The category involved is that of sacred writings, documents, and tenets. The data to be used are history, dogma, theology, beliefs, and the like. Essentially, both these suggestions are impersonal, focusing upon subject matter rather than upon its source, its use, or the persons for whom it is intended. Neither the divine nor the actively human is assured attention. This principle, in actual practice, lends itself to indiscriminate concepts of the Word of God, is often literalistic, seldom succeeds in conveying what it intends, and is tenuously related to life's concerns. Centering upon doctrine exalts a derivative rather than the Word from which it is derived, and in practice lends itself to the riding of dogmatic hobbyhorses.

There are those who think that the center of attention should be on the solution of life's problems. While problem-solving is a valid and useful method of instruction, as a center of attention it emphasizes disconnected human experiences. Its data are crises, personal concerns, and group concerns. Problem-solving can act well as a starting point and a means for Christian education, but not as a guiding principle. A method can never be successfully exalted in this way. Of course education deals with problems, but the prior question is, " What problems? "

Others propose that Christian education concern itself centrally with " life," experience, or the child. A life-centered Christian education would be mainly concerned with the ongoing stream of life's events and relationships. This would represent a commendable attempt to be realistic and " down to earth," but it is too vague and amorphous to be used as a guiding principle, and can give no real direction to the curriculum. Concerning an experience-centered Christian education, it needs to be said immediately that " the changing needs and experiences of the person " *is* the *organizing principle* for the curriculum, but it is always " experience in relation to something." It is the aspects of the environment with which the person interacts in experience that give experience its character. A child-centered education (aside from the obvious age-level limitation) does succeed in pointing out that attention *must* be centered on the learner, but again, it is always " the learner in relation to something." The data for each of these categories are the human experiences of the person, a dynamic educational suggestion, but one that is vague, in that it leaves the questions of " What experiences? " and " For what purposes? " unanswered. In fact, these categories only succeed in raising the question they are supposed to answer, since they all (life, experience, and the person) need to discover a guiding principle for their successful use.

There is a vigorous group of Christian educators who are convinced that the field should center upon the church. This idea has much to be said for it, yet it lends itself to concentration on the affairs and concerns of the church as an institution or as merely a human community. It can become absorbed in leading a person to understand and participate in the church's cultic and organizational aspects, thus tending to indoctrinate in symbolism and the development of institutional loyalty if it neglects that which calls the church into being. Actually, strictly speaking, such an emphasis can narrow Christian education down in unwarranted fashion to concern with certain limited areas of human experience to the exclusion of other areas of experience that are necessary for the Christian faith and life. Its successful use would assume other categories — God, the Bible, doctrine, social responsibility, and the like.

A large segment of those in Christian education would like to see Jesus Christ himself singled out as the central element, and speak of a Christ-centered Christian education. This is very close to the heart of the matter, for it properly exalts God's revelation and man's Redeemer. Yet, while Jesus Christ is the Lord of the church, and thus the Lord of Christian education, the idea of Christ-centered education can very easily be used in such a way as to neglect to put proper emphasis on the human side of the learner and his life, needs, problems, and achievements. Furthermore, its use often leaves the Christological question unanswered, so that the question of who Christ is may be answered by some in terms of the concept of the Jesus of history alone, and by others in terms that are merely doctrinally and not experientially Christological.

These proposed centers for a guiding principle have been examined mainly in terms of their adequacy, assuming that this criterion must be met in any case, and that the criteria of simplicity and clarity would be applied only to a suggested guiding principle that had first been judged completely adequate.

We have come so close to the discovery of an adequate element on which to build Christian education's guiding principle that the search need not go much farther. Is there an element that will be the very soul of theology, and yet so dynamically personal and transforming that it is indispensably educational? Is there an element that will bring the Bible, Christian doctrine, all human problems, life, experience, the child, the person, the church, and the Redeemer of mankind all into bold relief? I believe that there is such an element, and that it is the gospel of God's redeeming activity in Jesus Christ. My conviction is that Christian education can center in the gospel and use the gospel as its guiding principle with assurance of its complete adequacy, both theologically and educationally, and with assurance of its simplicity and clarity.

Our next task is to try to arrive at an understanding of the gospel, to propose a guiding principle that is centered in the gospel, and to evaluate that principle for adequacy, simplicity, and clarity. Then we can proceed to the development of a theory of Christian education in terms of objectives, curriculum principles, and principles of administration, all in the light of the gospel. In doing so, we may be confident that the theory will be one that will be adequate, and as simple and clear as possible — that it will thus be worthy and at the same time communicable to the volunteer leader and to the learner.

AN OUTLINE OF A THEORY
OF CHRISTIAN EDUCATION

[7]
The Gospel and Education

A t the same time that it is the responsibility of Christian education to be the church's effective servant, it is also up to it to be in a position to know and to contest the inroads of the cultural situation at the necessary points. To do this, it needs a theory that is adequate, both theologically and educationally. That theory, in order to be useful, has to be expressed in terms that can be readily understood and grasped by everyone involved in Christian education, including the layman and the learner.

In order to be readily communicable, the whole theory may well be informed by a guiding principle that is at once adequate, simple, and clear. This guiding principle can give Christian education sure direction by infusing its objectives, its curriculum principles, and its principles of administration. It will also focus the various elements that make up Christian education (all the concerns of the Christian faith and the Christian life), so that their meaning and use will be unmistakably clear.

It has been variously suggested that elements like the Bible, Christian doctrine, problem-solving, " life," experience, the child, the person, the church, and the person of Christ might serve as the basis for such a guiding principle.

The element that seems, however, to hold most promise of being able to focus the other elements, to give unmistakable guidance to Christian education, and at the same time to be adequate both from a theological and an educational point of view, is the gospel.

It appears, then, that the most promising clue to orienting Christian education theory so that it will be both worthy and communicable is to be found in recognizing and using the gospel of God's redeeming activity in Jesus Christ as its guiding principle.

The suggestion that the gospel be used as the basic guide for Christian education theory is supported by five arguments:

1. Revelation — the Word of God — is central in Christian education theory.

2. The gospel — God's redeeming activity in Jesus Christ — is the very heart and point of the Word he has spoken to men in their self-centered helplessness throughout the ages, and the very heart and point of the Word he speaks to men today.

3. The gospel is the clue to the meaning of history.

4. The gospel is the clue to the meaning of existence.

5. The gospel is the reason for the church's existence: it brings the church into existence; it sustains the church; it informs, directs, and corrects the church.

After discussing each of these points, we will be in a position to see whether the gospel can be properly used as the basis for a guiding principle.

1. *The Word of God*

In *The Task of Christian Education* (Chapter 6), after pointing out that in ordinary speech a word is a way of getting something across so that it will be understood, I discussed the Word of God as God's way of getting himself, in the most complete sense, across to men:

" The Word of God is God's attempt to get the nature of his being and his will across to us so that we shall understand it. Of course, it is more than the spoken word. As a rule, we regard the Word of God as not so much spoken as written, written in a book. But this again is not by any means the whole concept of the Word. Look again at ordinary words and you see what is involved. To help people to understand something you can show them what it is; you can tell them what it is; and you can make it possible for them constantly to be reminded of it. God uses all these methods: demonstrating, telling, and reminding us of his nature, existence, and truth. He shows us what he is like; here is the Word made flesh, Jesus Christ, pre-existent, existent in history, and eternally existent as the living Christ, the living Lord. He leaves us a written record of what he is like; here is the Bible, the Word in written form. Furthermore, he continually illumines our understanding of what he is like; here is the testimony of the Spirit to the Word within our hearts."

The Word of God is revelation. It is God's disclosure of himself, his revelation of himself.

In a deep sense the Word of God is spoken to us; God discloses himself to us. We have the opportunity and the responsibility to listen, to understand, to answer, and to become and do what is clearly implied. This is a dynamic encounter, by the very nature of the Word not so much an encounter with an idea or proposition as an encounter of a person-to-person kind.

Because we are rational beings, and always try to think out the meaning of our experience by translating it into ideas, we respond to the Word of God by trying to explain to ourselves and to other people what the encounter means to us. This gives rise to theology and doctrine, the formulation of the Christian faith. Let us come directly to the point — What is the Christian faith? What is our interpretation of our encounter with the Word of God?

The Christian faith has a source; its doctrine of God speaks to this matter. It deals with a problem; its doctrines of man and sin explain what this problem is. It believes that the problem has been solved; the doctrines of the covenant, the incarnation, the atonement, and the living Word attempt to explain how God has dealt with and solved the human problem. It believes that God has entrusted his work in the world to his people, and that he guides them by his Spirit; here it develops its doctrine of the church, including the church's ministry of the Word and sacraments and the church's mission. Christian faith has a goal; its belief about its goal is the subject of its doctrine of the fulfillment of personal destiny and human history. God's revelation of the meaning of life and history is thus the source and subject of the Christian faith.

It has been amply demonstrated that such an understanding of the Christian faith is absolutely indispensable to a theory of Christian education that is theologically worthy. Any Christian education theory that did not make this central would be distorted and would lack permanent value. Revelation, and the Christian faith as the witness to revelation, are thus central to Christian education theory.

The purpose of Christian education has often been glibly and superficially described as " to teach people about God." In a deep sense, this *is* the purpose of Christian education. And if it is, then the Word of God — his telling us who he really is — is the very heart of it. And the theological witness to the Word is of major importance in enabling men to listen to the Word, understand, answer, and become and do what is demanded.

2. *The Gospel — the Heart of the Word*

To a person or to a world so wrapped up in itself that it has never considered such a possibility, the fact of God's having revealed himself, the fact that in so doing he has revealed the meaning of life and history, the fact that he has made the human problem clear and has solved it, comes — if it does not seem like utter foolishness — as news, *good* news, *the* good news.

The New Testament writers saw in Jesus Christ the climax and fulfillment of the whole drama of history and revelation. The fact of who he was and what he did was the best news that man had ever received, or could ever receive. Such phrases as " the Word made flesh " and " the living Word " are a sort of symbolic shorthand by which the tremendous significance of the gospel is indicated.

The definition of the term " gospel " in the concordance of *The Westminster Study Edition of The Holy Bible* (The Westminster Press, 1948) is this: " The word means ' good news,' ' glad tidings.' Hence it is used of the message proclaimed by Jesus himself concerning the coming King-dom of God, and then of the story of God's redeeming activity through the life, death, and resurrection of Jesus Christ, proclaimed by the apostles and recorded by the Evangelists."

The gospel is the Bible's essential unity, since it is the gospel that the Old Testament anticipates, and since it is the gospel that constitutes the message of the New Testament. At its climax, according to Millar Burrows (in *An Outline of Biblical Theology;* The Westminster Press, 1946), the Old Testament proclaims the expectation of the gospel:

> " Failure to do God's will as he has revealed it incurs judgment; but God does not leave the guilty without

hope: he offers the undeserving sinner redemption and reveals the way to obtain it. The promise of the new covenant includes forgiveness. This note sounds strongly in the later prophets, especially Second Isaiah, who again and again proclaims the good news of deliverance. This is the origin of the Christian word "gospel." The law shows what God requires and the penalties of disobedience; the gospel shows the way of deliverance when man has failed to meet the requirements. This is what Paul means by justification, God's free gift to the sinner."

The gospel constitutes the message of the New Testament. In his analysis of the word "gospel" (in *A Theological Word Book of the Bible,* p. 100; The Macmillan Company, 1950), Alan Richardson says:

"After the death and resurrection of Jesus the content of the gospel, as it is understood by the apostolic church, is Christ himself. It is no longer simply 'the gospel of the Kingdom of God' (though, of course, that is involved), but is 'the gospel of Jesus Christ, the Son of God' — a phrase in which every word must be given its full significance. It is 'the gospel of God,' the saving message which God has addressed to the world, first by way of anticipation in the Scriptures, and now finally in the living Word, Jesus Christ. It is therefore supremely the message of the cross and the resurrection, and it is 'the power of God unto salvation to every one that believeth.' The church itself is built upon this one gospel and is indeed a fellowship in the gospel. The gospel must always be received personally by faith. For those who thus receive it the gospel is always 'news,' breaking in freshly upon them and convincing them afresh, though they may first have heard it and accepted it long ago." (Used by permission.)

It was in the mid-1930's that, browsing in a bookstore on upper Amsterdam Avenue in New York, I came across

Principal Alex. Martin's *The Finality of Jesus for Faith*
(T. & T. Clark, Edinburgh). The book had been written
in 1933. It was a period when the churches were given to
" religiousness," or to a combination of literalistic pedantry
and sentimental emotionalism. Into such an atmosphere
Principal Martin's direct witness to the gospel came with
intense clarity. It has been my polestar ever since. He
points to the gospel as " the supreme service rendered to
men by Jesus." That service, he says, does not consist:

". . . in instruction alone; and it is only less inadequate
to put Him forward as exhibiting a pattern to be repro-
duced. He does more even than introduce a new ethico-
religious type into history. What he assumes to do . . .
is different in kind from this. The word for it is ' reconciliation.' . . . He redeems from the most intimate and
grievous of all the contradictions of the human lot, the
distress and slavery of sin. Through him, and above all
through his death, his followers find harmony with the
world, restoration to fellowship with the Power at the
heart of it; and with that is given the assurance of vic-
tory and peace. It is a matter of experience that morally
distracted souls do thus find the readjustment with Reality which they crave. They do, in plain spiritual fact,
pass into "the Holiest of all " — to the very heart of
Existence where alone spiritual nature can rest — through
the rent veil of this Man's flesh. They consciously draw
nearer very God the more they become one with the
dying Jesus, entering more deeply into his consciousness
of the hateful thing that brought him to his end, acknowledging with him submissively the righteousness of
the divine reaction against it, and taking hold with him
believingly of the mercy — discovered in the cry, ' Father,
forgive them, for they know not what they do ' — that
nevertheless is over all.

" To express it otherwise: theological terms and Biblical figures and modes of speech apart, what is it, in bare
spiritual simplicity, that Jesus has achieved for men?

. . . In the case of a sinless nature it might perhaps be [possible to have] a free spiritual fellowship with the living God in trustful obedience and love [without Jesus]: in the nature we know, darkened, degraded, distraught through evil . . . the fulfillment of the divine purpose in our life is hindered fatally. Only Jesus helps men here, and above all in his dying. As they identify themselves with that dread experience, believing men find themselves reunited with the spiritual order they belong to; the will is restored to freedom which had willfully become unfree; and deliverance is experienced from the impotence and disability of every kind which had followed on that. Since, in and through the dying Jesus, they come into contact with That in which he lived and moved and to whose care he at the last committed himself, and find it to be a living Power of Love bent on reversing the course of natural consequence, forgiving sin, and eliminating its power from life." (Used by permission.)

Thus, the gospel — God's redeeming activity in Jesus Christ — is the very heart and point of the Word he has spoken to men in their helplessness throughout the ages, and the very heart and point of the Word he speaks to men today.

3. *The Meaning of History*

The gospel is the clue to the meaning of history. God deals with man through the medium of history. The perception of history and historical relationships is man's God-given way of finding himself and the meaning of his life in the continuum of time.

Meaningful history is, looked at from a thoroughly realistic perspective, the account of God's relationships with man. History *past* is the story of what he has done with, for, and through man. History *present* is his current activities with, for, and through man. History *future* is what he intends to do with, for, and through man.

Suddenly, then, the Bible, with the gospel as its major motif, comes into perspective as "holy history." In this context it is clear that through his relations with the Hebrew people God *indicated* his redemptive purpose in history. Through the birth, life, death, resurrection, and ascension of his Son in history, he has *established* his redemptive purpose in history beyond the shadow of a doubt. In the same events he has *guaranteed* the victorious conclusion of his historical activity.

When the redemptive activity of God makes itself known to a man or a people it comes as *the* good news. Thus the gospel of Jesus Christ is God's revelation of the meaning of man's historical life.

Cultures rise, flourish, and decline in history. Their achievements and their conflicts are historical. In each culture, whatever its achievements or conflicts may be, the church is God's historical instrument, with a message to deliver. It is the gospel that constitutes the message that the church has to deliver to each historical culture, else how can the culture know the meaning of the history of which it is a part?

4. *The Meaning of Existence*

But look at the matter, not from the perspective of the long sweep of God's purpose in history, which may seem very remote and impersonal, but from the perspective of the individual life, one's personal existence.

God's redemptive purpose seems to *me* to be very far removed unless *I* am involved in it. My immediate existence consists so largely of the world of my private thoughts and feelings that I tend to perceive my surroundings in terms of the patterns into which I have channeled my subjective needs. I do see what is around, but unwittingly I see it the way I want to see it, the way I am habituated to see it.

Yet I want to live, and to live fully. As I try to do so, I seem to be prevented from it. The great desire of my heart, the thing that will make my life complete, is within my grasp. But even as I reach out for it, it eludes me. Or, if I do succeed in grasping it, it turns out to be not what I thought it would be, and is hardly worth the having.

I realize that what prevents me from living fully is that I see everything essentially from only one vantage point, and that from within. The world turns out to be not what it seems because my apprehension of it is completely distorted by my own desires, my preconceptions, my habits — in a word, by my whole point of view.

Someone tells me that what prevents me from living fully is my sin. Not so much the wrong things I do — they are more results than causes — but a whole warped attitude toward life. The universe as I see it revolves around me. I need to get outside myself, to gain perspective, to see things in *true* proportions and relationships.

Then the enormity of the situation dawns on me. It is arrogantly presumptuous of me to look at life as I do from my human, personal, egocentric point of view. I have simply been ignoring God. I have dethroned him from my life. My sin is thus radical sin, and deserving of death. This deserved penalty I would have to pay for having ignored and dethroned my God.

At the depth of my predicament I hear of the incarnation and the atonement (or I hear of the manger, the teacher, the healer, the cross, and the empty tomb). Then the overwhelming point of a sentence that perhaps had become obscure because of my having used it too much or too early speaks to me — " God so loved the world that he gave his only Son, that whoever believes in him should . . . have eternal life."

And as I respond, the old *I* does die, and He gives me a new birth of life in him.

This is *the* good news. Thus the gospel of Jesus Christ is God's revelation and living achievement of the meaning of existence, even of individual, personal existence.

5. *The Gospel and the Church*

In discussing the church and its educational work, I said that the church is the human instrumentality brought into being by God in Christ to continue his ministry of redemption to the world. Plainly, the gospel was and is the soul of that ministry.

The gospel is the reason for the church's existence. The reality of the gospel, its power, and the imperative for its communication brought the church into being. The gospel sustains the church in performing its functions (as outlined in Chapter 7 of *The Task of Christian Education*) in every generation and in every culture. The gospel, as the church's essential message, informs, directs, and corrects the church.

Thus, in a situation where the church and the culture are in tension (as they always are to some degree), it is the church's business to communicate the gospel. The gospel is what the church says to the culture. The church knows something that the culture does not know but needs to know. It is the work of the church to employ every means to deliver that urgently needed message.

The church's own members live in the tension between the church and the world. If they are, in this situation, to perceive, accept, and fulfill the gospel, every means must be employed to help them to grasp it in all its implications.

To those outside the church's fellowship the gospel must also be communicated by every available means, that they too may perceive, accept, and fulfill it, if that be God's will.

THE GOSPEL AND EDUCATION

One of the ministries by which the church communicates the gospel to its members and to those outside is the ministry of teaching. The teaching function of the church is:

1. To deliver the message that in man's extreme need God has forgiven and redeemed him in Jesus Christ. This is urgent.

2. To help those inside and those outside the church to prepare themselves for response to that message.

3. To show them how to respond.

4. To help them to see and work out the fullness of the implications of the message of the gospel for themselves and their world.

If one way by which the church communicates the gospel is by teaching, then the gospel is of central concern to Christian education. Because it sustains such a vital relationship to the church's teaching ministry, there are certain specific connections between the gospel and Christian education that can be pointed out, bringing the whole matter into focus at this point.

Christian education (defined in the fullest sense to include the church and the Christian home) has a task of preparation for response, demonstration of how to respond, and guidance in mature response as it seeks to make persons aware of their living encounter with the gospel.

In *In One Spirit* (p. 17; Friendship Press, 1958) I put it this way:

> "The individual has his choice. He may remain in tragic bondage to self, society, and culture. This is what is meant by "the human predicament." On the other hand he may become a free person, by God's Spirit, through his response in complete devotion to Jesus Christ. Christian education seeks to prepare the individual to respond in faith by the power of the Holy Spirit, to show him how he may respond to the living Word as it is spoken to him, and to guide him into increasingly mature and effective ways of responding to the Holy Spirit and doing the Father's will. This is why Christian education is called the nurture of the Christian life." (Used by permission.)

The emphasis is clearly on how one becomes a free person through response to the gospel.

This, in turn, makes it even more evident than before that Christian education in the church (again, using the term in the fullest sense) is responsible for assisting persons to perceive the gospel, to accept it, and to see its demands and fulfill them. There is never a time in a person's life or in the life of the church when any one of these aspects may be separated from the other two, but it is helpful in seeing the church's educational task with persons of different levels of experience to point out that in childhood the emphasis is likely to be more on perceiving the gospel, in youth on accepting it, and in maturity on discovering and meeting its ever-changing requirements.

Thus Christian education definitely implies the closest attention to the gospel and to its work at every point. When we examine the objectives of Christian education we will see them in the light of the gospel. When we look at educational procedures, it will be chiefly in the context of the gospel. And when we describe the educational programs and institutions involved (including church and home), the major concern will be with communicating the gospel and nurturing faithful discipleship in the light of it.

Christian education is inextricably bound up with the gospel, but what of education in general? Here, again, some things that have been said before come into focus. Education has to be concerned with helping persons to see things as they are and to come to grips with life. Its indispensable emphasis is on human becoming — the development of free and mature persons. We have seen how the various aspects of so-called secular education — technical education, liberal education, and moral and religious education — can be carried on in the light of the gospel if the learner approaches them from a fully Christian perspective. Something of the results of that approach in increased insights, higher achievement of competence, and a greater sense of having come to terms with life, have been hinted at.

The teacher in so-called secular education, as well as the learner, can do his work within a Christian perspective. If the gospel is what it claims to be, it involves living relationships and a quality of life even more than it does the use of any particular words or the expression of any particular sectarian ideas. The teacher who, in a secular school, lives and teaches in the assurance of God's redeeming love for him in Jesus Christ, provides a living witness that needs no special words in the classroom. Such a teacher need not, indeed cannot, hide who he is, how he became what he is, what he does as a result, and what it means to him. His whole life, from personal devotions to responsible social action, girds him for his witness.

But the words themselves need not be missing. They

cannot be the subject of exhortation in the public class-room. Yet it is the responsibility of every teacher, and especially teachers of subjects dealing with the expression of human needs and values, to point out, among the various approaches to the problems of life, the fact that there is a Christian gospel, and that it provides a distinctive approach to understanding and dealing with human problems.

These are some of the relationships of the gospel to education — both church education and education in general. Consideration of these relationships has brought us to the place where we can summarize the possibility of the gospel as the criterion for education. Is it adequate? Is it simple? Is it clear?

The gospel provides an adequate basis for guiding Christian education because it is integral to the Word of God, because it is the clue to the meaning of history, because it is the clue to the meaning of existence, because it brings the church into existence and gives it its imperative, and because (in educational terms) it is the clue to human becoming.

The gospel provides a simple basis for the guidance of Christian education because, for all its profundity, it may be put in a simple proposition (God's redeeming work on man's behalf in Jesus Christ) and in concrete terms (as concrete as the manger, the teacher, the healer, the cross, and the empty tomb) without losing anything really essential.

The gospel provides a clear basis for the guidance of Christian education because it is easily and readily understandable at many different educational and experience levels.

THE GUIDING PRINCIPLE STATED

Conceived as a principle that may be used to assist and guide in the development of objectives, curriculum principles, and principles of administration, this center and focus on the gospel in Christian education may be stated thus:

If Christian education will focus its attention on the gospel, it will be properly oriented and conceived. Around the gospel the other elements of Christian education may be grouped, but it is the one element that can stand alone and give the others meaning. The gospel is the essential element in establishing the institutions of Christian education and devising their curriculums.

Here then, in the form of a guiding principle, is summarized the conviction that the central concern of, and norm for, the educational life and work of the church is the gospel — in all its implications for the revelation of God, for the nature and condition of man, for the meaning of history, for individual and social salvation and responsibility, for the significance and mission of the church, and for the fulfillment of human destiny.

[8]

Educational Objectives in the Light of the Gospel

THE GOSPEL can do for us the most important service that Christian education needs. It can help us to set our objectives. It can help us to devise our curriculum. And it can help us to build an administrative setup that will be an appropriate and effective means for doing the church's work.

In and through this service, the gospel can help us to speak tellingly to our culture. The basic problem is that of the communication of the gospel to people in our times. Even the realization that this *is* the *basic* problem is a great help. As we live in Christ and, by the power of the Holy Spirit, in the community of believers, the gospel becomes clearer to us as the message that we as the church have to deliver to the world. *What* we have to communicate thus becomes gradually clearer.

As we live perceptively in our world, learning its language and its ways, we discover what its actual assumptions about the meaning of life are. We also find out what its consuming and pervasive values are. Its ways of life and its modes of expressing its values become known to us, even as we share them. We begin to get clues to the approaches to use, the " language " involved, and the process of mutual sharing that is called for in communicating with our world and culture. Thus we begin to see *how* the message of the gospel may be expressed for our day and for the people with whom we are dealing.

At the same time, because all this means that insights into the gospel and insights into the culture and its values have interpenetrated and shed light on each other, we perhaps have begun to be aware that in the strictest sense we are not in a position to communicate the gospel on our own at all. What we are in a position to do is to become human channels by which God will, if he chooses, realize the work of grace through the gospel. The work of the apostle, the prophet, the evangelist, the pastor and teacher is a gift. (Eph. 4:11.) We are given the gospel and the power to communicate it. In the deepest sense he who is to proclaim the gospel, in whatever mode, becomes a free man by becoming the gospel's servant.

This is how the use of the gospel as the guiding principle for Christian education can help us. It can give us direct guidance in Christian education practice. It can help us to speak to our culture. It can itself become clearer and more meaningful to us as we thus use it, putting ourselves at its disposal.

EDUCATIONAL OBJECTIVES

We turn now to the first specific problem of Christian education theory — the problem of constructing educational objectives in the perspective of the gospel. When we were considering how to build a theory of Christian education, we said several things about objectives that may now be reviewed and brought into focus.

We said that by objectives is meant the purposes, goals, and intentions of Christian education; that the objectives of Christian education are used to guide the planning of the curriculum; that the results of both curricular and administrative efforts are to be evaluated in terms of these goals; and that satisfactory use of the foundation disciplines would call for asking three questions of those disciplines: What categories of objectives are called for? What shall the aims be in each of those categories? How shall these aims be employed?

First, then, we will try to discover what kinds of objectives are needed. Then it will be necessary to get historical perspective on goal-making, both in education in general and in Christian education, in order to see what the present situation is with regard to Christian education objectives, and what the present situation means. When we have gained historical perspective, and have determined the status and meaning of the present purposes, we will be in a position to deal with the question of providing the purposes that are needed.

What kinds of objectives are needed? Look at a class engaged in some aspect of Christian education. In the classroom are pupils and a teacher. They are engaged to some extent consciously in an enterprise of the church, and they are to some extent aware that what they are doing has to do with God.

The pupil brings into that classroom a multiplicity of personal aims, engendered by his needs, and expressed in terms of inner motivations. Religion comes into the picture when the pupil becomes concerned with questions of identity (who he really is), relationships (with what and whom is he connected, and to what and whom is he responsible?), universal meaning (what is life's real and final explanation?), and purposes (what is he seeking, and why?). The pupil's aims are powerful, even though they may not really be formed in his own mind. In the classroom they are sometimes unknown to the teacher and to the other pupils, sometimes ignored, sometimes explored, sometimes used, sometimes met, and sometimes changed. I would venture to say that these are the most important, if also the most elusive, aims of Christian education. The success or failure of the whole enterprise depends upon the degree of real guidance focused on them.

The teacher's aims are likely to be the most obvious ones in that classroom. The imperative to teach religion carries with it certain aims on the part of the teacher as an individual — to help make the pupil aware of the gospel, for instance. It also implies other aims on the part of teachers as a group — department aims, age-level aims, and sequences of aims from one achievement level to another.

Pupils and teacher together are trying to work toward achieving the aims of the church. They are trying to find out what the church is, what their relationship to it is (individually and as a group), and what their responsibilities are within it, to it, and because of it. Because it is a church with a heritage, it expects that heritage to be taught. Since it is a church with a message, it expects that message to be delivered. And because it is a church with a program and mission, it expects enlistment and participation in its purposes, life, and work.

The most unusual thing about that classroom is the thing that is least obvious and most important. There are clues to it in the kind of studying that goes on, the fact that there is worship, the peculiar situation in which both pupils and teacher seem to be looking and listening for something, and in the pervasive atmosphere of prayer. Those involved seem to be aware of something, seem to expect to be shown something, seem to expect to hear something. The secret is, of course, that in the classroom where Christian education is taking place there is to some extent awareness of God and awareness that the important thing is to discover and do his will.

Christian education takes place as God's will, the church's purposes, the teacher's goals, and the pupils' aims are acknowledged, weighed, and blended. The first and major classroom task is the reconciliation of all these objectives, and the planning of classroom activities in the light of the result.

The example used has been that of the classroom, since it provides a common and well-recognized setting for Christian education objectives. Extend your idea of Christian education beyond the classroom in the church to the club meeting, the evening youth group, the home, the public school, the summer camp, the counselor's study, the pupil's own room, or to any of the other myriad points at which Christian education is now known to take place, recall all the persons and institutions involved, recall that every person involved is growing and changing all the time, and you see some of the complexity of the problem of objectives in Christian education. The task of blending all the objectives involved into something that can be understood, planned for, and guided looms up as a very difficult matter.

With the illustration of the classroom situation, and the reminder of the complexity of the problem, we are at a point where perhaps we can be fairly analytical and discriminating as to the categories of objectives that are needed. They run the whole gamut of concern in Christian education.

There are, first of all, those objectives which the individual and the group hold. They emerge out of the situation, needs, interests, and duties of both the person and the group or groups to which he belongs. These are individual and group *motivations,* and are to be known and dealt with as such.

Again, there are the great realities of the Christian faith and the great concerns of the Christian life. These include marked centers of attention within the whole field of divine-natural-human-historical relationships. Such matters as our relationship to God, our relationship to Jesus Christ, our concern for social order, and the like, immediately suggest themselves. These great Christian realities and concerns have most often been singled out for attention as objectives in Christian education. Actually, they constitute the great *themes* of Christian education, and are more useful in analyzing the content of the educational relationships involved than they are in indicating the goals of those relationships.

The great themes of Christian education, dealing with the realities of the Christian faith and the concerns of the Christian life, are most often subdivided so that concentrated attention may be given to their various aspects in some combination of logical sequence and psychological sequence. This is where *topics* and *problems* fit into the picture of objectives.

In any group situation involving education the persons working together will in some way set the *goals* for their common enterprise. These are usually in the form of some combination of long-term and short-term aims. Often different persons within the group will be moving toward different goals, but the educational enterprise is planned in such a way that the goals will be co-ordinated and that the achievement of these different goals will result in mutual enrichment.

The teacher and parent are often eager to know whether

the pupil has attained what should be expected of him. The learner himself is likewise interested in checking his progress. This is the function of the age-level objective. In my judgment, the psychological basis for the concept of age-level objectives, however, is untenable. I would like to see substituted for that concept a new one involving *levels of progress* related to sequences of developmental experiences within the context of the great themes. That is, instead of asking, " What should a junior's experience of Jesus Christ be, and how does this pupil's experience compare with the standard? " I should prefer to ask, " In the developing sequence that may be expected in the individual's experience of Jesus Christ, where does the pupil's experience fall at the present time? " In other words, I would be willing to entertain the possibility of something like standard sequences of experiences, but would not be willing to see a particular level of experience irrevocably nailed down to a particular age level.

Furthermore, there is the actual *learning task* that the individual or the group undertakes as a means of gaining the knowledge, skill, attitude, or idea that is desired. In a real sense the task itself becomes an objective.

In one way or another, then, the goals of Christian education take the form of individual and group motivations, the great themes of the Christian faith and the Christian life, specific curricular topics and problems, goals that teachers and pupils set together to guide their enterprise, stated levels of progress, and learning tasks that are undertaken.

The construction of educational goals in the context of the gospel calls, however, for co-ordination and unity among these various kinds of objectives. A more discriminating use of terms may be called for. What is needed is *a basic objective* in terms of which all these others will become meaningful and useful to Christian education.

THE HISTORY OF OBJECTIVE-MAKING

The construction of objectives in Christian education has been of great concern since the 1920's, and has been under constant study. The process has been deeply affected by what has been taking place in education in general in the field of objectives. A brief review of events and trends in education in general will shed light on the Christian education problem.

Herbert Spencer set the tone for the consideration of educational aims in the nineteenth century with his key question, " What knowledge is of most worth? " Efforts to answer the question eventually went beyond " knowledge," strictly speaking, until in 1912 and 1913 the Commission on the Reorganization of Secondary Education enunciated the influential " Seven Cardinal Principles," which became the main objectives of secondary education for the period. The emphasis, for all that it had broadened, remained tied to the subject matter to be taught.

In the 1920's, however, a new movement became prominent, led by Franklin Bobbitt and W. W. Charters. They felt that the objectives of education should be reflections of the things people needed to know, the skills they needed to perform, and the qualities they needed to possess in order to meet their duties in society satisfactorily. The aims of education should thus, in a sense, be based upon the job analysis that indicated the person's actual and expected duties. This led to the setting of objectives in terms of the laborious analysis of all the areas of human experience and the functions involved in each.

Here we may shift attention to the field of Christian

education objectives, for it was under the research chairmanship of W. W. Charters that the International Council of Religious Education launched its work on the International Curriculum of Religious Education in the 1920's.

The International Curriculum (which was abandoned before completion) was based upon the analysis of the areas of human experience involved in being Christian. It was felt that " being Christian " might be defined in terms of certain character traits agreed on as Christian, and that the task of Christian education was to help the individual to develop these traits in all the areas of his experience. The curriculum was to consist of " units of guided experience " designed to develop these traits.

The director of research for the International Council at this time was Paul H. Vieth. He not only directed this enterprise but engaged in an investigation of what recognized leaders in the field considered to be the objectives of religious education. His study of objectives proved to be more enduring and influential than the work on the curriculum itself.

The International Council, rightfully impressed with Vieth's work on objectives, considered his list, added one objective to it, and officially adopted the resulting eight objectives to guide the Christian education work of American Protestantism. There has never been a more influential list than this:

" Christian education seeks to foster in growing persons a consciousness of God as a reality in human experience, and a sense of personal relationship to him.

" Christian education seeks to develop in growing persons such an understanding and appreciation of the personality, life, and teachings of Jesus as will lead to experience of him as Savior and Lord, loyalty to him and his cause, and will manifest itself in daily life and conduct.

"Christian education seeks to foster in growing persons a progressive and continuous development of Christian character.

"Christian education seeks to develop in growing persons the ability and disposition to participate in and contribute constructively to the building of a social order throughout the world, embodying the ideal of the Fatherhood of God and the brotherhood of man.

"Christian education seeks to develop in growing persons the ability and disposition to participate in the organized society of Christians — the church.

"Christian education seeks to develop in growing persons an appreciation of the meaning and importance of the Christian family, and the ability and disposition to participate in and contribute constructively to the life of this primary social group.

"Christian education seeks to lead growing persons into a Christian interpretation of life and the universe — the ability to see in it God's purpose and plan, a life philosophy built on this interpretation.

"Christian education seeks to effect in growing persons the assimilation of the best religious experience of the race, pre-eminently that recorded in the Bible, as effective guidance to present experience." (Used by permission.)

It is evident that this list falls into the category of what I have called the great themes of the Christian faith and the Christian life. It stood for many years, and its validity and usefulness were reaffirmed when it was incorporated into the International Council's statement of basic philosophy, *Christian Education Today*, in 1940. The present statement, *Goals for the Christian Education of Children*, reflects the point of view of these objectives.

With the growing theological concern, and with changing conceptions of curriculum patterns, the need for re-study was felt. The Study of Christian Education, in the mid-1940's, in which Vieth was very influential (see Vieth, *The Church and Christian Education*), set the stage for the present emphases on theology and education in Christian education, and made it obvious that some revision of objectives was called for.

The Committee on Junior High Objectives was the first to produce a formulation that was more consciously theological. (*Junior High Objectives,* 1953.) By the time its report was published, the International Council had been merged into the National Council of Churches. The report was brought out under the new auspices.

In the meantime, a committee had been set up for the revision of the general objectives, a committee was actively working on a statement of goals for senior high work, and the revision of the objectives for children's work was being planned for.

The revised statement of general objectives is now before the denominations, referred to them by the National Council of Churches. The heart of the statement is a " supreme purpose " that is similar to the " basic objective " of the National Council's study paper on senior high objectives (see below). The statement of general aims then goes on to list five areas of experience with which Christian education must deal if the supreme purpose is to be accomplished.

The study paper on senior high objectives (National Council of Churches, 1958) abandons the use of the term " objective," except for its use in connection with the basic objective of Christian education. In spite of the fact that it began with the intention of formulating " senior high objectives," the committee early came to the conclusion that there is one objective for Christian education, and that the one objective is shared by all regardless of the age-level concerned. The objective of Christian education, as developed in *The Objective of Christian Education for Senior High Young People* (copyright, 1958, by the National Council of Churches), is as follows:

> " The objective of Christian education is to help persons to be aware of God's self-disclosure and seeking love in Jesus Christ and to respond in faith and love — to the end that they may know who they are and what their human situation means, grow as sons of God rooted in the Christian community, live in the Spirit of God in every relationship, fulfill their common discipleship in the world, and abide in the Christian hope." (Used by permission.)

One can see immediately the new place given to one basic objective in Christian education, and the relation of what I have called the great themes to that objective. Mainly oriented to Christian experience as theology sees it, and thus centered in the gospel, the new statements of purpose are beginning to show some promise of a reconciliation between the profundities of theological understanding and the valid findings of the science of education.

To indicate the interest and ferment in this matter, one need only recall that recent studies along this line have been issued by the Presbyterian Church U.S.A. (*Basic Principles, Christian Faith and Life;* Board of Christian Education, approved by the General Assembly, May 26, 1947), The Methodist Church (*Educational Principles in the Curriculum;* General Board of Education, 1952), the United Lutheran Church in America in co-operation with other Lutheran bodies (*The Objectives of Christian Education;* Board of Parish Education, 1957), and the Presbyterian Church U.S. (*Christian Education Within the Covenant Community — the Church;* Board of Christian Education, 1958). Other denominations are likewise engaged in the clarification of objectives.

Providing the Objectives That Are Needed

We have seen the kinds of " objectives " that are needed: motivations, great themes, topics and problems, pupil-teacher goals, levels of progress, learning tasks, and a basic objective to give them all focus and meaning. All these must reflect God's intention, and must thus in some clear way be centered in the gospel.

If, however, all are developed extensively, and " from the ground up," one can predict that on the basis of past history's judgment the result will be confusion. Furthermore, that confusion will be compounded by the fact that, being so various, their individual status will be very questionable.

If, on the other hand, all are informed by the gospel as their guiding principle, then they will be clear, and the way is open all along the line for flexibility and change (which are completely necessary) without losing Christian education's essential moorings.

The heart of the matter lies in the careful enunciation of the basic objective, and its use in connecton with the others for guidance and evaluation. Here I find the basic purpose as stated in the National Council of Churches' senior high document to be as satisfactory as any statement yet made public.

It may be of interest to point out that in 1929 the papal encyclical *The Christian Education of Youth* contained this statement: " The proper and immediate end of Christian education is to co-operate with divine grace in forming the true and perfect Christian, that is, to form Christ himself in those regenerated by Baptism."

An intriguing aspect of the matter has developed. We said that one of the questions to be answered was, " What shall be the objectives in each category? " Clearly there are many objectives that cannot be anticipated in any standard way, but that by their very nature come into being as the situation demands, and cease to function once the particular need that brought them into being has passed away.

This is true of many motivations, although constant attention can be given to anticipating and planning for certain motivations. The great themes can be definitely determined, although their analysis into topics and problems need not necessarily be done in any standard way. Pupilteacher goals cannot be anticipated except by setting down ranges of goals from which particular ones might be selected. Levels of progress can be developed definitely in terms of sequences within the great themes, but the work on this has scarcely been started. Learning tasks may be indicated in an inclusive way from which particular tasks may be selected within fairly standard categories. (See the National Council of Churches' senior high document for the most thorough study of learning tasks in Christian education to date.) The basic objective of Christian education, however, may be stated quite clearly in terms of the centering of the process in the gospel, and may then be used to guide and check all the rest of the various kinds of objectives.

HOW ARE THEY TO BE EMPLOYED?

Objectives have two uses — to point the way, and to provide standards for evaluation. Look briefly at the various categories of objectives, and the application of these uses becomes evident.

It is the function of the motivations of the individual and the group to shape up the approach to Christian education and to determine emphases and effort. They are not of much use in evaluation, since by the time evaluation is appropriate they are either used up or redirected.

It is the function of the great themes of the Christian faith and the Christian life to provide the comprehensiveness that is required in Christian education, so that no important dimension or center of attention is missing. Topics and problems serve to make the use of the themes specific, thus pointing the way in a definite fashion. Teacher-pupil goals do the same, and also serve admirably as criteria for evaluation.

It is the function of the levels of progress to act as standards for evaluation, and in so doing to point the way for future planning. This is especially important since they are set within the context of sequences of developing experience.

The learning task serves primarily a planning purpose, although the measurement of the accomplishment of the task is an important evaluative matter.

The basic objective is the key to the situation. Its function is to provide " direction and perspective for the whole process. Its strength is its drawing power — its ability to give unity, direction, and selectivity to the entire educational plan. The basic objective is thus the objective for every learning task, every lesson, every unit, every meeting throughout the curriculum." (From the National Council of Churches' senior high document.)

[9]

Educational Procedures
in the Light of the Gospel

WE HAVE dealt with the need for theory in Christian education, showing how the condition of the culture, the imperative of the church, and the process of education all require it. Further, it has been shown how a theory may be built, and built in such a way that it is communicable. A guiding principle, making the gospel central to Christian education, has been shown to hold real promise for the construction of theory. How that guiding principle may be used in the construction of the objectives of Christian education was outlined in the last chapter.

It is now necessary to go on to the development of curriculum principles and principles of administration with the gospel as the central structure. This chapter will concentrate on educational procedures and the next on educational programs and institutions.

A SYNOPSIS OF THEORETICAL RELATIONSHIPS

Before turning directly to the consideration of educational procedures, however, it will help if we take a total look at Christian education theory as it is beginning to emerge. This is in the nature of a bird's-eye view before filling in more of the detail.

We are now in a position for the first time to do this,

since all the essential relationships have been established, and especially since the objective has been stated.

With the objective as the starting point, we can proceed to define the setting in which Christian education does its work. Then we can analyze briefly the setup that the church uses for doing its educational work, and what it does in and through that setup in order to reach its objective. This, in effect, is the total concern of Christian education — its whole theoretical outline.

This can all be said in three " nonstop " sentences. Here are all the essential parts of Christian education, shown in proper relationship to one another. (The first, seventh, and eighth paragraphs are taken from the National Council of Churches' senior high document.)

Objective: The objective of Christian education is to help persons to be aware of God's self-disclosure and seeking love in Jesus Christ and to respond in faith and love — to the end that they may know who they are and what their human situation means, grow as sons of God rooted in the Christian community, live in the Spirit of God in every relationship, fulfill their common discipleship in the world, and abide in the Christian hope.

Setting: Since Christian education takes place in a field of relationships consisting of the natural, the human, the historical, and the divine;
Since persons in our day live in a culture that interprets the field of relationships in pluralistic, dynamic, complex, secular, and scientific, ways;
And since the gospel is the heart of the redeeming Word that God has spoken to persons in this or any other culture;

Administration: Therefore the church, in its program and institutions of Christian education, through formal activities, informal activities, and encouragement to private religion;

Curriculum: Provides opportunity for engaging in the life it lives and the work it does through study, creative expres-

sion, action (witness, service, social action), fellowship
(group living, outreach), stewardship, and worship;
In which persons listen with growing alertness to the gospel
and respond in faith and love, explore the whole field of
relationships in the light of the gospel, discover meaning
and value in the field of relationships in the light of the
gospel, appropriate that meaning and value personally, and
assume personal and social responsibility in the light of the
gospel.

Objective: All of which, by the power of the Holy Spirit,
evokes response to the love of God, guides persons in
growth as children of God, and gives them the sense of
membership and mission that comes with faith in Jesus
Christ.

CURRICULUM THEORY

It is evident from the analysis of theoretical relationships, as indicated in the synopsis, that the curriculum consists of selected educational procedures used to further the
achievement of the aim of Christian education, and that
it is devised for use by various agencies of Christian education (the Sunday church school, youth groups, etc.).

Curriculum materials are those printed (and other) resources which contain the suggestions and wherewithal for
the procedures that become " live " curriculum when they
are put into use with the persons and groups for whom
they are intended. Methods, on the other hand, are the
educational activities employed in the curriculum.

The curriculum's educational procedures are to be
thought of, then, in terms of experiences through which
learning may take place. Subject matter is employed at
every point, but always in the context of changing and developing learning experiences. The teacher may think that
his is a purely subject-matter course, unit, or curriculum.
But the fact is that he is in such a case making a critically

important, if unconscious, assumption — that the learner will automatically experience the subject matter involved in such a way as to assimilate it. Thus experience, the learner's experience, is always at the root of the matter in curriculum.

The new and revised curriculum materials of various Protestant denominations, the publication of *A Guide for Curriculum in Christian Education* by the National Council of Churches, the concentrated attention to the revision of Christian education objectives, and the vigorous promotion of leadership education, are all evidences of the renewed interest of the Protestant churches in curriculum matters. They indicate that there is, in Christian education circles, a felt need for vital thinking on curriculum theory.

The presence and consciousness of this need for constructive work on curriculum theory calls for concerted efforts in many quarters. All such work should contribute to an increasingly productive conversation on the matter. I included some important guides to curriculum thinking in Chapter 14 of *The Task of Christian Education,* but did not attempt to construct a systematic theory.

I am concerned here to outline the content of curriculum theory. When the process of building a theory of Christian education was discussed, it was said that in the area of curriculum principles ten questions need to be put to the foundation disciplines. The ten questions that were then listed will be dealt with now, one at a time.

1. *What are the curriculum's distinctive contributions to the accomplishment of the task of Christian education?*
Christian education's task is the nurture of the Christian life. This is done, in actual fact, in many places, under

many circumstances, sometimes in planned ways, and sometimes in unplanned ways. The curriculum consists of the planned activities taking place under the aegis of various agencies like the church and home, through which Christian nurture may be undertaken.

It thus becomes the responsibility of those charged with the planning or conduct of the curriculum to take into account quite realistically the objectives of Christian education, the learners involved, the agencies and groups working together, and the resources available, and to do a thorough and creative job of working out the kinds of learning experiences that will be appropriate and adequate.

2. *Are such principles as comprehensiveness, balance, sequence, and flexibility valid for curriculum building?*

These four principles have often been suggested, in one way or another, as the basic principles for the curriculum of Christian education. What do they mean, and how valid are they?

Comprehensiveness means guaranteeing the inclusion of every essential element. Balance means guaranteeing that every element will get proper emphasis without sacrificing any other element. Sequence means the determination of the steps by which Christian learning may take place, and the planning of the curriculum so that those steps may be taken at the appropriate points. Flexibility means guaranteeing adaptability in terms of the educational settings where the curriculum is to be used, in terms of method, and in terms of individual, community, and cultural differences.

The sufficiency and soundness of these principles may be determined by taking five factors into account. The five factors are the learner's native equipment (any curriculum principle must be realistic about the hereditary background of the learner), the learner's world (any curriculum principle must take society, culture, the contemporary scene, and nature into account), how the learner grows (the developmental picture), what the learner seeks (motivation and motivation theory), and how he learns (learning and learning theory).

Comprehensiveness is a matter of the learner's world and his growth. Balance and sequence are concerned with his world, his growth, what he seeks, and how he learns. Flexibility is a problem comprising all five factors.

These five factors are so important for educational procedures that some analysis of them is called for. I will deal with the last two, since the first three I have worked on rather thoroughly in Part Three of *The Task of Christian Education.*

What is the basis for education so far as motivation is concerned? Understanding a motive as a unique combination of thought and emotion (" the power to put an idea into action," for instance) and closely bound up with the will, we are ready to inquire as to the possibility of any standard analysis of motives that could be used as a basis for the planning of education.

The motivations that may be counted on for curriculum purposes might be outlined as qualities persistently sought in human living. They might well be:

> Health
> Relatedness
>> Sensitivity
>>> Knowledge
>>> Creativity
>>> Wisdom

>   Responsibility
>   Membership
>   Fellowship
>   Usefulness
>   Ethical living
> Integrity

These are stated as abstract qualities. They are actually made up, at any given point in a person's life, of very specific experiences and relationships.

What is the basis for education so far as learning theory is concerned? Modern psychological theory suggests that we learn in four ways: through perception, through practice, through problem-solving, and through identification.

Learning through perception is a blend of insight and discrimination. It is a matter of finding patterns (insight) and signs or cues (discrimination) in the field of experience. The learning takes place when the learner is encouraged to explore a situation (is taken into it systematically) until he sees its inner organization and its essential signals, and until he sees what it means — grasps or " understands " it. Then he is encouraged to make it his own through seeing detailed relationships and meanings within it, becoming skilled in responding to it and dealing with it, and using it in the right ways. Once he has the key to the situation he is at home in it and can (usually rather quickly) make it pretty completely his own.

Learning through practice is essentially a matter of training. Traditionally, it makes use of Thorndike's " laws " of readiness, exercise, and effect, although these have been greatly modified both by Thorndike himself and by other theorists of learning. " All learning is a process of establishing mental connections, ' bonds,' between stimuli and responses. This is done by massive repetition with appropriate rewards when the learner masters or associates the right response to the right stimulus." Although this represents the most influential form of this theory, there are those who question both repetition and rewards, while holding to the general outline.

Learning through problem-solving assumes that the person will learn when he is presented with a situation that is somewhat baffling and has to find his way through it. In the process it is believed that he learns to think, and that he " learns " the resources he has to use to solve the problem. The procedure is, as a rule, to define, analyze, suggest possible answers, select the most promising ones, gather the facts, weigh the answers in terms of the facts, choose the best answer, test it in action, and evaluate it. By this time several new problems will have popped up that will need solving.

Learning through identification involves " the appropriation into the self of the characteristics of an admired group or person " (*Dictionary of Education*) . The learner associates and classifies himself with the admired group or person and through analysis, imitation, worship, and the like, incorporates into his personality the desired qualities. Recent studies have shown that values are effectively " interiorized and internalized " through identification.

Our task in Christian education curriculum would seem to be to try to be clear about what we want to teach — being inclusive and rather profound about it, excluding nothing — and to sort it out as well as we can according to the things that may best be learned through perception, the things that may best be learned through practice, the things that may best be learned through problem-solving, and the things that may best be learned through identification. Then we can pick our methods and procedures accordingly.

Enough has been said in connection with this question

to show how profitable a thorough analysis of these five factors would be for the validation and enrichment of the basic curriculum principles, and for the whole process of Christian education.

3. *What elements are to be included in the curriculum?*

The elements to be included in the curriculum consist of the indispensable centers of attention in the whole field of natural-human-historical-divine relationships. These constitute what we have called the great themes of the Christian faith and the Christian life.

Any list of the elements of Christian education must be so constructed as to be comprehensive, but at the same time so as to reduce those elements to the real essentials. One of the reasons for this is that the field is too great to be comprehended without careful selection of centers of attention. Another reason for careful selection is that in practice Christian education has the task of focusing all of life's experiences and concerns on the really important matters; consequently it is these few matters that are its distinctive concern, while they are of such a nature that they call the whole field to mind and give it meaning.

The statements of objectives cited in the last chapter clearly imply certain elements. The guiding principles that were considered for Christian education indicate what some might be. The various denominational curriculums are all based upon carefully selected elements. The curriculum, *Christian Faith and Life,* uses as its chief elements Jesus Christ (the Lord of Christian faith and life), the Bible (the Scriptures in Christian faith and life), and the church in Christian faith and life (including its history, program, and mission); it groups every aspect of instruction around these.

The officially adopted program areas for youth work (Christian faith, Christian witness, Christian outreach, Christian citizenship, and Christian fellowship) are another splendid example of the attempt to be completely comprehensive and yet give pointed enough direction for the curriculum.

In discussing the guiding principle for Christian education, I enumerated on page 88 what appear to me to be the major elements that cannot be omitted.

One of the perpetual research tasks of Christian education theory is the reconstruction of its conception of its elements. Here is one of the major points at which the foundational disciplines may quite evidently be of indispensable assistance.

4. *What organizing principle shall be used to guarantee the curriculum's unity?*

If the elements of the curriculum were to be used as "subjects of instruction," and if the curriculum were to be built simply by putting them one after the other in some kind of order, the result would be complete lack of coordination and unity. In view of the comprehensive nature of the curriculum, some organizing principle is needed that will help to give proper weight to the various elements at every point as the curriculum develops, that will guarantee balance, and that will provide continuity.

A glance back over the various lists of elements is enough to give the essential clue. Quite clearly, all these elements are intended to be of personal meaning to individuals and groups. They are used, whatever their inherent value, in the context of the developing experience of the individual and the group, in order that their meaning and value may be known and apprehended.

When The Study of Christian Education stated the organizing principle for Christian education curriculum, it
was done in precisely these terms. " The organizing principle for the curriculum is the changing needs and experiences of the pupil, in relation to . . ." (There followed
a list of the other elements of Christian education.) It is
important to note the significant fact that the organizing
principle is in terms of needs and experience, but always
in relation to something or someone to be experienced.
Here is the key to comprehensiveness with practical and
effective curriculum organization, and without diffusion
and irrelevant sequence.

If the organizing principle is the changing needs and
experiences of the pupil, then the curriculum becomes a
matter of listening with growing alertness to the gospel
and responding to it in faith and love, exploration of the
whole field of relationships in the light of the gospel, the
discovery of its meaning and value in the light of the gospel, personal appropriation of that meaning and value, and
assumption of appropriate personal and social responsibility in the light of the gospel throughout.

By listening with growing alertness to the gospel and
responding to it in faith and love is meant hearing, accepting, and fulfilling the demands of the gospel. This means
becoming aware of God's self-disclosure and seeking love
in Jesus Christ and responding in faith and love, experiencing the transforming and reconstructing power of the
Spirit. One becomes aware of the gospel by taking part in
the worship, life, and work of the church, by studying the
Bible, and by praying. When repentance is followed by
acceptance of the gospel, the receiving of it and dependence
upon it, then growth takes place in realization of its implications and demands throughout the whole field of

relationships. Discoveries and personal appropriations of meaning and value are reviewed, re-examined, and reconstructed in the light of the gospel.

By exploration of the field of relationships in the light of the gospel is meant getting to know it in that light. This involves getting acquainted with the world, human interests, and human concerns; gathering information; and gaining rich and varied experience.

By discovery of meaning and value in the field of relationships in the light of the gospel is meant understanding and appreciating it in that light. This involves reflecting on experience, sorting it out; seeing relationships, systematizing them, and testing them; and arriving at a point of view and a set of values.

By personal appropriation of that meaning and value is meant making them one's own. This involves experiencing the transformation of ideas into convictions, philosophy into loyalties, and values into a way of life in the light of the gospel.

By the assumption of appropriate personal and social responsibility in the light of the gospel is meant doing things about what one has discovered and made one's own. This involves putting convictions, religious imperatives, and life values to work in the world around.

The person's needs and experiences, as the organizing principle of the curriculum, thus make possible the full use of the gospel as the guiding principle and center, and provide the realistic means by which the gospel may become the focus of the whole field of relationships.

5. *How shall objectives be used in the curriculum?*

Objectives, as indicated in the previous chapter, are used primarily for guidance in curriculum building and for evaluation of the results of curriculum work. It was shown there how different kinds of objectives have different values in these connections, and how the basic objective has the major responsibility for serving both these functions throughout the whole process.

6. *How shall the curriculum be designed?*

Curriculum design is a matter of the selection and organization of content which is defined here as the experiences of persons in relation to the various elements of Christian education.

Selection of content is made by carefully combining, under the guidance of the Holy Spirit, the areas of experience in the field of relationships (the great themes, or the elements of Christian education) with appropriate kinds of experience (like listening and responding to the gospel, exploration, discovery of meaning and value, personal appropriation of meaning and value, and assumption of responsibility).

Content is usually organized by deriving and building cycles, units, and lessons in such a way as to provide for comprehensiveness, balance, sequence, and flexibility.

The curriculum is thus designed in terms of (1) the themes involving the realities of the Christian faith and the concerns of the Christian life, translated into topics and problems, and (2) the learning process, in which teacher and pupils together set goals, make plans involving specific learning tasks, carry out the plans, review, evaluate, and set new goals.

Here it should be noted that both teaching units (consisting of specific lesson plans) and resource units (collections of materials from which specific lesson plans may be devised by different teachers) will be much more valuable if they will suggest a range of goals (all possible avenues toward the objective) from which particular groups might choose the one or more that are most appropriate to their situations. In curriculum design, however, no attempt should be made to have the suggested goals add up cumulatively to the achievement of the basic objective. Nor should they be derived by segmenting the objective. It is the function of the basic objective to inform and " draw " every aspect of the curriculum, including every unit. It operates " whole " throughout the entire process and in every educational situation. There is no equation between the objective and the sum of proximate goals.

7. *How shall curriculum materials be built?*

Questions of the format of curriculum materials are to be dealt with on the basis of several considerations: prior decisions on the selection and organization of content, the institutional requirements of the groups for whose use they are intended, the experience and achievement levels (as well as the specific interests) of the persons who are to use them, feasibility in editorial production, and feasibility in commercial production and marketing.

These curriculum materials are coming to include not only periodical materials like teachers' and pupils' quarterlies, but also reading books, projected and nonprojected visual aids, recordings, and various other kinds of instructional objects.

8. *Who shall be responsible for curriculum building?*

Curriculum building may be taken to have two meanings. There is the building of the experiences that constitute the educational process; this is a matter in which a number of responsible parties share, including teachers

and the pupils themselves. This might be called the building of " live " curriculum. There is also the building of
curriculum materials, which is a matter of the preparation
of various items, including systematic suggestions for lesson procedures, that will be useful to many persons and
groups in the process of building live curriculum. Here
the concern is to discover who is responsible for the building of both these aspects of curriculum.

One of the critical spots for the building of live curriculum is the local church. Decisions that are made and
put into effect in its various groups will determine to a
large extent what happens in Christian education and how
effective it is. Teachers, pupils, superintendents, and members of boards and committees on Christian education have
to take the initiative and work together on this. Not often
do they do curriculum building without help, since their
job usually begins at the point where they select and put
into effect some particular series of printed materials. But
from that point on, the adaptations and adjustments that
really spell success or failure in curriculum are up to them.

Another critical spot for the building of curriculum is
the home. If the most effective Christian nurture takes
place in the home, as is often suggested, then the careful
building of the conditions and experiences of nurture
becomes a central task for parents and other members of
the home. Little has been done at this point, although
there is a growing consciousness of need.

Various community agencies — scouts, clubs, the public
schools, and others — take upon themselves tasks that are
closely related to some aspects of Christian education.
Character education, citizenship education, education in
moral and spiritual values, and teaching about religion are
some of the more obvious of these. These agencies and

the churches would do well to come to some mutual understanding as to what is to be done in these areas, and why, in order to avoid conflict and achieve unity and co-ordination as far as possible.

The responsibilities of the denomination for curriculum building are for the most part in the area of producing and servicing curriculum materials. It is the denomination's job to determine basic policies in terms of sound theory; to make decisions as to form; to have materials written, edited, and produced; to market them; and to help to guarantee their proper use through consistent and thorough training of leaders.

The responsibilities of interdenominational agencies have become clearer of late years. They are not to produce curriculum material — except for certain missionary education and audio-visual productions. They are to provide the opportunity for the hammering out of curriculum policies and the preparation of basic curriculum outlines. They are also charged with the conduct of certain aspects of the leadership-training task, especially where it involves experimentation with new or unusual methods and materials.

The key to curriculum building, however, is in the learner himself. It is the course of study that he builds for himself — made up of experiences of his own that may very well have been suggested by the curriculum that others have built on his behalf — that really educates. As was said before, possibly the most important objectives of Christian education are the real motivations of the individual and the group. These are where the live curriculum is built, and here is where Christian education is made or broken. The learner is ultimately responsible for his own study and his own education.

9. *How shall the curriculum be evaluated, and by what criteria?*

The question of the evaluation of curriculum presents one of the most difficult problems for Christian education. When should the curriculum be evaluated? How should it be evaluated? By what criteria should it be evaluated?

Curriculum materials should be evaluated at several points. The theory behind them needs scrutiny. So do the original outlines and plans. The editors need to evaluate the writers' work carefully, and to keep on evaluating with careful and thorough judgment until the materials have finally gone to press. Then, after they are used, they need to be looked at again judgmentally in order to provide for improvement when they are revised.

Live curriculum also needs evaluation as it is being planned, as it is being carried through, and after it has been finished. The evaluation of live curriculum may, however, interfere more than it helps. A plant needs to be allowed to grow before it is inspected and judged. Too much premature evaluation may disturb the process and prevent growth.

The way to evaluate a course of study is usually through some co-operative process that includes all persons responsible. The most telling evaluation, then, is that done by learners and leaders. It involves knowledge of the materials and plans, keen observation of the educational process in operation, summarizing of results, mature reflection on all three — plans, process, and results — and the drawing of measured and useful conclusions. These conclusions are, in turn, fed back into the planning process.

What shall the standards for curriculum be? In the fullest sense, the standards are its objectives, always scrutinized critically in terms of the basic objective. Both written materials and live curriculum must measure up to theological and educational standards at every stage, and must also be looked at carefully from a functional point of view.

The application of theological and educational standards means judgment in terms of the best of Christian education theory. The application of functional standards means judgment in terms of the effective use of the materials and processes to motivate; encounter and explore new problems and possibilities; set personal goals; set group goals; enable the individual to unbend and be himself; break down artificial barriers within a group and enable it to do its work in an atmosphere of mutual regard, trust, and helpfulness; participate with others in productive give-and-take; gather and sift information; use information and develop skills through discriminating practice; retain information and skills through repetition; gain insight; reach personal conclusions; express needs, feelings, conclusions, and values creatively; express needs, feelings, conclusions, and values socially; serve the needs of others; and witness.

10. *How shall proper use of curriculum materials be guaranteed?*

Practical guides are needed for administering and servicing curriculum materials. For instance, curriculum materials should be selected only after it has been decided that the particular materials will be of real assistance in meeting the Christian education needs and achieving the Christian education objectives of the persons and the church concerned.

Furthermore, an adequate setting must be provided for the use of curriculum materials. The conditions for their use, so far as building, equipment, and prevailing atmosphere are concerned, must be met.

Able and trained leadership is essential. The leader

should know his materials from objectives through to methods. He must be able to translate curriculum materials into live curriculum. He must do so carefully and conscientiously from session to session, seeking to meet the needs and to guide the experience of his particular students intelligently in the process. There also must be an understanding that is common to all leaders as to the purposes of the curriculum and the procedures to be used so that each will know and do his particular part.

It is necessary as well that the pupil be oriented to the curriculum materials and guided in their use. If the curriculum is actually to be organized around his changing needs and experience, he cannot be treated as if he were only the recipient of the process in a passive way. He must be brought in as an active participant. This means making it clear to him what is to be done, what materials are involved, and why. It also means keeping him abreast of developments as they are expected and planned to take place, and guiding him in participating in them. The more he can himself help in planning for the use of curriculum materials, the closer he will come to playing his most creative and effective role.

◇

The answers to these ten questions constitute the outline of a curriculum theory. To the extent that it is guided by the central principle of the gospel it evidences proper concern for the individual, assumes the proper role and mission for the church, suggests the proper content in terms of experiences, shows the proper relationships among the various elements of content, and suggests the proper use of content.

It is only an outline. The further work that needs to be done is the development of a richer and more obvious connection between its every proposal and the foundation disciplines by which it must be fed and judged. The contributions of these disciplines have scarcely been tapped, yet the use that has been made of them here shows how valuable they are to the enterprise.

Consider now in the light of one of the foundations — the church's life and work — the methods that are involved in the curriculum of Christian education.

METHODS OF CHRISTIAN TEACHING

What is a method? It is a form of systematic procedure for accomplishing an educational task. It is an activity used in learning. Thus a Christian education method is a means or plan for getting some aspect of the Christian education job done. Materials (including equipment, supplies, lesson materials, and the like) may be thought of in this connection as the wherewithal for methods.

The heart of method is to engage in the life the church lives and the work it does. It is the living of the Christian life, under experienced guidance, as it is most appropriately lived at each stage of the individual's development.

We learn discipleship by being disciples under the guidance of those who are experienced in it. We learn to worship by worshiping under the guidance of experienced people. We learn Christian social responsibility by taking responsibility as Christians under the guidance of persons who are themselves socially responsible Christians.

No method will open God's word to us unless it teaches us to read, to listen, to hear, to decide what his word means for us, and to live accordingly. Effective method here depends upon doing these things and associating closely with those who can give out of the fullness of their own experience the kind of direction that will keep us from making mistakes or getting off the track.

The Bible, church history, and doctrine remain essentially secular until the living Word breaks through to us in Christ, and living in him we need the record of his revelation, the perspective of the history of his church, which is now ours also, and the guidance of the structure of systematic truth. In a deep sense the real teacher and guide in Christian education is God himself, and the methods of education are those that he chooses to use.

We believe that God's word and gospel tell us how he deals with men, what his intentions and methods are. We see the heart of his method in the ministry of Jesus Christ, in the atonement, in the choice of a New Israel, and in the giving of the Holy Spirit. For us this means that our methods must be chosen to accord with his redemptive purpose, to accord with his gift of the Spirit, and to accord with his centering of responsibility in the church that he has chosen.

The method of Christian education is thus to *be* the church of Jesus Christ. God has called the church into being as a witnessing fellowship. It expresses its witness in the many aspects of its life.

Christian education will take place, for instance, if the church school class is the church of Jesus Christ. It will occur in the worshiping group and in the praying cell. It will happen in the nursery at play, in the kindergarten on a visit to the organist's loft, in the junior department making its time line or painting its missionary mural. It will take place in the session as it threshes out the question of whether or not the members of the mission chapel shall be welcomed into the membership of the parent church and the mission chapel building closed. It occurs in the board of trustees as next year's budget is worked out and in the youth group on its play night.

The clue to method is the church as a community, a fellowship, carrying on its work in creative relationship to its living Lord, and involving every child, youth, and adult in that work and in that relationship.

It is not the church unless it is at work. The various types of work it carries on (study, creative expression, action, stewardship, fellowship, and worship) involve methods of Christian education. In fact, they are the prime methods of Christian education.

The church of Jesus Christ is a studying church. It searches the Scriptures in order that it may hear, understand, and obey the word of God. It reads church history in order that it may be wise in judgment on its own life, that it may know rightly why it exists, that it may know its unity and variety, and that each member may participate and know himself to be part of the ecumenical church. The church studies doctrine in order that it may rightly divide the word of truth, have a reason for the faith that is in it, and be able to answer the questions of the age. It looks at modern man, the modern world, and their problems and the practical questions of living that it faces and that its members individually face. The invasion of the world by the gospel requires understanding of the world. Christian discipleship implies growth in self-understanding.

The church of Jesus Christ finds itself and says what it means through creative expression. It uses music and the other arts to express and communicate its faith. In its hymns, anthems, literature, liturgy, architecture, windows, and paintings it says for itself and others what its faith is and what it means. Creative expression is a proper mode for the church to use in its education from the earliest ages onward, since it offers such a variety of " language " and opportunities to say what is really meant. Every mode of experience, from listening to the gospel to the assumption of responsibility, is involved in the use of the creative arts.

The church of Jesus Christ is a church of action. It witnesses, engages in mission, and undertakes social action. It criticizes, suggests, serves, and nurtures prophetic living. Its action is co-ordinated with its study. The world is its laboratory for the trial of truth.

The church of Jesus Christ practices the stewardship of time, talents, and resources. Its aim is faithful service to its Lord, and that faithful service requires that the means at its disposal be cared for and used to the best possible advantage to further its witness and mission.

The church of Jesus Christ practices and is fellowship. " God in Christ not only binds men to himself and opens to them the joy of communion with himself; he also binds them to each other in love . . . [in a] fellowship of faith. . . . It is the community of faith, the family of God, that from the very creation God has been seeking to bring into being upon earth, and it is in this community of faith that God means each Christian to have his life. . . . The church should be a family, a family of faith in which the members know and understand each other, and education into the church is growth in one's full participation in the family." (James D. Smart, *The Teaching Ministry of the Church*, pp. 122–125; The Westminster Press, 1954.) Thus fellowship includes both group living at its fullest and outreach that seeks for all the fellowship of faith.

The church of Jesus Christ is a worshiping church. Parents initiate the life of prayer and worship. The nursery provides the link to the church as a worshiping fellowship. The order of service itself is instructional as well as inspirational. We learn to worship as with integrity we participate in worship and have its significance interpreted for us.

As the church engages its members, and others who are listening to and beginning to respond to the gospel, in its work of study, creative expression, action, stewardship, fellowship, and worship, it is the church doing its educational work. These are the means that are intrinsic to the church and thus are the heart of its educational procedures. They are the ways in which Christian education may proceed with nurture in the light of the gospel.

[10]

Educational Programs and Institutions in the Light of the Gospel

I N OUTLINING a theory of Christian education in the light of the gospel, attention has been given to the determination of objectives and to principles of educational procedure. The third major area of theoretical concern has now to be considered — that of educational programs and institutions.

It has been suggested by Charles Duell Kean (in *The Christian Gospel and the Parish Church;* The Seabury Press, Inc., 1953) that the life of the parish itself may be an experience of the gospel. He gives as illustrations ways in which such matters as judgment, justification, and salvation may be actual experiences in the life of the parish church. The point that he makes is that this is real Christian nurture; it is the church actually knowing itself to be the community brought into being and living its life in the gospel. No one sociological type of parish or community is implied; it is essentially a matter of relationship to the gospel rather than any particular type of structure.

Can it be then that administration itself may be carried on in the light of the gospel? It would seem that this is not only a real possibility but an imperative. If this is possible, then the setting is provided for the answering of the three questions on administration. How and by whom shall the program be planned and organized? How and by whom shall the program be managed? How and by whom shall the program be supervised, that is, standardized, evaluated, and systematically improved?

PROGRAMS AND INSTITUTIONS

Why are programs and institutions necessary? The Christian church uses programs (including educational programs) in order that its responsibilities may be discharged systematically. It uses institutions (including educational institutions) in order that its work may be done in an organized way with regularity and continuity.

The chief educational programs and institutions with which we are concerned are those of the local parish. In the ordinary church these will include work like that of the church school (the Sunday church school, the vacation church school, the weekday church school), the youth fellowship, communicants classes, scout groups, missionary organizations, women's organizations, men's organizations, and other activities.

In addition, the institutional picture includes agencies that serve beyond the local church. The first large group of such institutions includes schools and colleges (mission schools, church-related colleges, and theological seminaries). The second group includes the various service organizations (denominational boards and interdenominational agencies) that have been set up to assist in various ways with the administration of Christian education.

The programs and institutions in the local church and beyond are constantly under judgment. They are never free from the question of what they are accomplishing. The frank answer to the question is that they are accomplishing a great deal, but that their accomplishment does not seem to be at all consistent across the nation; not even consistent from church to church within a denomination or community; not even consistent from group to group or from class to class within a given church; not even consistent from year to year within a given group or class.

Accomplishment by the various agencies of Christian education seems to be conditioned by their segmented nature, their tendency not to " add up " to a program that can be seen and understood clearly. Their effectiveness seems to run all the way from the excellent to the worthless or even harmful.

Faithful and intelligent administration in the light of the gospel could, conceivably, give direction and point to the church's educational programs and institutions. The condition of inconsistent accomplishment might thus be somewhat improved.

ADMINISTRATION

Administration makes use of all the processes by which a rich and unified program of Christian education is provided for all ages. Its functions are organization, management, and supervision.

Organization is the process of setting up the program. It gives special attention to grouping and to leadership. Management consists of the performing of all the functions necessary to the effective operation of the program. Certain aspects of superintendency are included in management, as well as the secretarial function, the financial function, and custodial service. Supervision requires the performance of all the functions that go into seeing that the program is of the highest possible quality. These include standardizing (arriving at norms descriptive of the detailed goals and characteristics of the program for each organization, department, or group), evaluating (comparing what is with the standards and determining adequacy and needs, using surveys, tests, and other types of measurement), and improving (following up the discovery of needs with the practical steps that may bring the program and structure up to standard).

We said that it is not only possible but imperative that administration be carried on in the light of the gospel. Administration centered in the gospel is administration that cannot exist for its own sake, but seeks at every point to be a channel for the communication of the gospel. The administrators of Christian education have themselves accepted and are seeking to fulfill the gospel. The structure of the administrative groups is under constant scrutiny, and subject to change, to make it more effective in doing its job. The principles upon which administration operates are permissive and enabling, so that the channels for the gospel's work may be definite but not rigid. It thus guides itself by principles that are functional, democratic, and co-operative.

Since the term "democratic" has been introduced it should be noted immediately that democracy in administration means definite location of authority and responsibility, but with every encouragement to communication and participation in policy-making. The governing body of the local church is usually the one that has ultimate responsibility for the administration of Christian education. Its authority is sometimes partly delegated to a committee on Christian education, which in turn delegates certain specific responsibilities to particular administrators (superintendents, and others).

If such a committee on Christian education is set up, its task is the creation and maintenance of a unified educational program in the church. Its major functions are research, study, planning, policy-making, counseling through supervision, leadership selection and training, extension, and curriculum recommendation. No aspect of the educational life of the church is outside of its jurisdiction.

The creation and maintenance of a unified educational program in the church can perhaps be accomplished best by the committee on Christian education if it is conceived on a broad age-level basis. It is important not to become rigid or narrow in age-level divisions, but the broad division of the program into children's work, youth work, and adult work seems to be warranted. It becomes easily defensible if, in addition, the committee gives attention to family life in the church and to all-church activities in a unified way.

The main thing for the committee to keep in mind in building the church's program of children's work is that the central motif be that of perceiving the gospel. Children are usually defined as those eleven years of age and younger. The program of children's work consists of the Sunday church school, the vacation church school, the weekday church school, nursery school, Christian education in the home, activity groups, summer camps, and other miscellaneous groups and activities. The important policy considerations in children's work are that no activity be carried on under the auspices of the church that is not supervised by the church, and that all the children's work of the church be directly related to the achievement of the aim of Christian education on appropriate levels of perception. The work should be thoroughly and richly Christian in quality, and educationally sound. This calls for co-operative supervision of every phase of the work.

The main thing for the committee to keep in mind in building the church's program of youth work is that the central motif be that of accepting the gospel in the most penetrating sense. Youth are usually defined as those who are twelve through twenty-three years of age, although the upper limit varies considerably. The whole youth program (consisting of many varied organizations) is encompassed in the youth fellowship, whose program areas are Christian faith, Christian witness, Christian outreach, Christian citizenship, and Christian fellowship.

The main thing for the committee to keep in mind in building the church's program of adult work is that the central motif be that of fulfilling the gospel. Adults are usually defined as those twenty-four years of age and over. The adult program encompasses the whole adult study program, the training of church officers, young adult work (for those twenty-three through thirty-nine years of age), parent and family-life education, work with older adults (those sixty-five years of age and older), women's work, and men's work. In many ways the whole program of Christian education will stand or fall on the effectiveness of the program of adult work. The old notion that the church could start with children and not bother too much with adults has long since been shown to be completely false.

Much creative work remains to be done in the field of those program activities that cut across the age levels, especially family activities and all-church activities. Family-night programs, and even outings, are steps in the right direction. A beginning has been made in family camping. But the local committee on Christian education would do well to put all its imagination and resources to work at this problem.

One of the deep concerns of Christian education administration is that of criteria for determining the Chris-

tian orientation of its institutions. In March, 1955, at the
Executives' Conference of the Division of Educational and
Medical Work of the Board of National Missions, held in
Santa Fe, I was asked to lead in a consideration of the
marks of a Christian institution. Although the discussion
was ostensibly limited to the consideration of mission
schools, hospitals, and community programs, the breadth
of experience and wisdom of the missionary participants
produced results with far wider application. The group
started with a draft statement for consideration. This was
revised by a representative panel. Then in groups the
whole conference reworked the matter. The results from
the groups were not brought together in any final form,
but the panel's statement can serve as an indication of what
institutional and program administration of Christian education in the light of the gospel may be:

> "A Christian institution is called into existence by
> Christians in order to meet certain pressing needs. Its life
> span is only as long as those needs or other compelling
> emergent needs endure. Within its life span its life and
> program change, sometimes radically, in sensitivity to
> changing needs.
> "Its vitality depends upon the vividness of its Chris-
> tian experience, the integrity and quality of its program,
> and the maintenance of an essential focus outside of it-
> self. The institution finds itself by reaching out in serv-
> ice beyond itself.
> "The institution is integrally related to the church to
> the point of being the church, the Christian community,
> a laboratory for Christian living. Christian living per-
> meates the institution.
> "At every point (administration, organization, cur-
> riculum, method, student-teacher relations, and corre-
> sponding areas of health and welfare projects) the pro-
> gram and life of the school is Christian.

" It is not defined by a campus or a set of buildings, but by a group of people working together to meet a problem or get a job done.

" It adheres to and exemplifies the principle of love.

" It engages in a well-balanced variety of religious activities of a formal nature.

" It encourages in those it touches the impulse to church vocations and/or Christian service.

"It is a functional approach of the church using techniques and methods of modern scientific, sociological, and psychological discovery to unite man with man and man with God by love, as motivated and directed by the historic and ever-living Christ. That motivation it shares with all who become a part of its life." (Used by permission.)

Such an analysis expresses the kind of administrative policy for the church's program and institutions that puts the gospel at the heart of its work, and that attempts to remove the administrative hindrances that all too often in an institutional situation prevent the free working of the gospel.

LEADERSHIP

Probably the crucial administrative problem for the church's program of Christian education is that of leadership. The situation is that the Protestant church programs are operated by a vast staff of volunteer leaders (several millions of them, generally of high school achievement level), guided by a skeleton staff of professionals. The leadership called for is administrative, instructional, and for the oversight of semiautonomous groups. There is a thirty to thirty-five per cent turnover in such leadership annually.

A review of the kinds of leadership required makes the problem vivid. Leaders are needed for the church school

— superintendents, secretaries, treasurers, teachers, assist-
ants, substitutes, audio-visual counselors, nurses, and others. For youth groups, officers and advisers are needed. It
usually takes dozens of leaders of various kinds to run the
women's association. The same is true of the men's association. Include the home in the picture. Include also
camps and conferences, where volunteers of unusually high
quality are needed in increasing numbers.

The questions of securing, placing, and orienting leaders should be handled as parts of one process. Jobs should
be clear, and recruiting for them specific. They should be
arranged so that the leader may move around systematically as he becomes properly trained and gains the necessary experience. Variety and change should be carefully
planned for so that the worker does not get in a rut, on
the one hand, and so that the program is not disrupted, on
the other. There should be a systematic pre-service training
program, stressing both content and method, and so arranged that it will help to build up a reservoir of leadership potential. Every member should be regarded as having
some possibility of leadership service, but due regard
should be given to the fact that the qualities of " follow-
ership " are also important to develop.

This points directly to the principle that the leadership
training program should be for those who now serve (an
in-service training program), and for those who have leadership potential (a pre-service training program). It is a
shared responsibility of the local church, the churches of
a community working together, and the denominations.

The pattern of leadership education that has served
longest and very effectively is that exemplified by the
Standard Leadership Curriculum, which is a project of the
National Council of Churches on behalf of the denomina-

tions and local councils. The plan of the Standard Leadership Curriculum provides for courses designed to give background, content, and methods to the teacher. There is a carefully prepared catalogue of graded courses from which churches and community schools may make selections of the courses they need, a system of accreditation of instructors, and standard textbooks and leaders' guides.

One of the most effective techniques of leadership training, introduced several decades ago, is the laboratory school. Here the teacher-in-training watches a skilled teacher at work with a group of children or young people, has the process analyzed for him in accompanying seminars, has every opportunity to ask questions about what he has seen, and then gradually begins to take part in the teaching, with careful help in planning his work and evaluating it.

Another form of this kind of training is apprenticeship, where a new teacher helps an experienced teacher for a period of weeks or months before taking a group on his own. In many situations teachers and other leaders are encouraged to visit other teachers and leaders at work, after making suitable preparations for the visit. One denomination has set up a plan for selecting exemplary departments in various church schools around the country, which may be visited by arrangement.

One of the types of training that is rapidly growing in popularity and use is coaching, or previewing, as it is often called. This very practical approach permits the previewer to help the leader in his preparation for using the curriculum materials for the next lesson, unit, or quarter. Help here centers around the actual preparation of lesson plans. Coaching will be a much more effective technique when it is balanced by the use of the clinic method, where careful evaluation of past performance precedes planning for the future.

Personal supervision, one of the more difficult but very effective means of leadership training, is used with some frequency, especially where there is a professional director, or where the minister is trained to provide such service. This includes observation of the leader at work, and periodic consultation with him to evaluate and help him plan his work.

The "workshop" is now being introduced to the churches as a possible addition to the field of leadership education. It provides expert help, in the form of consultants, in the freest and most informal kind of atmosphere. The purpose of the workshop is to help each participant to put his finger on his real problem, and to get the help that he needs on it. Thus personal conferences, a great deal of individual reading, and much informal give-and-take are required. The really effective workshop is at least several weeks long, and is a residence affair.

Some of the traditional aspects of the Christian education program have real possibilities for leadership education. Much has been made of the possible transformation of the old teachers' meeting into a real workers' conference. With the present departmental curriculums, department workers' conferences have become absolutely necessary in most churches. The same possibilities have been cited in connection with workers' libraries in churches, but here the success of the project really depends upon having an alert librarian who knows the curriculum, and keeps the teachers in touch with resource materials that would be of help to them.

There has been some experimentation also with roving trouble shooters whose task has been to go from church to church to help with the servicing of the curriculum. There have also been a few cases in which the radio and television have been used in an area for leadership training.

Out of all these possibilities, traditional and new, there emerges a pattern that gives promise of real help on the matter. It is the demonstration-observation-laboratory school and practicum, which has been tried with some success. Here, as the term implies, is an expanded workshop type of situation in which foundations are carefully laid and objectives developed. Then the student watches experts at work in actual teaching situations. The student then does the teaching himself under the guidance and supervision of the experts, and from day to day evaluates and plans ahead under their guidance. This is an expensive and time-consuming type of program, but it has the distinction of assuring the training of leaders.

It is possible that the period just ahead in Christian education may be one in which there will be great advances in leadership education. If so, it will be because of some combination of the following trends, some of which have already begun to be felt:

A new definition of leadership as " co-ordinated effort toward group goals."

The growing realization that people learn to the degree that they participate. This means more use of the laboratory method.

The conviction that the most practical training correlates with denominational curriculum and program materials.

Increasing use of the media of visual education.

Greater co-operation between church-related colleges

and seminaries and their communities in leadership education.

Recognition of the need for both content and method in leadership education.

Growing recognition of the importance of the quality of life and personality of the leader himself.

An important factor in the leadership picture is the very slow but rather steady growth of professional leadership. There are now many types of positions open for professional service in Christian education. There is no possibility of the volunteer being displaced or replaced, but he may be able to have better access to help in his work than has been the case before.

Some of the types of positions in the field that have been opening up are that of the director of Christian education in the local church, the assistant in Christian education in the local church (college rather than seminary trained), the minister of education, the minister of youth, the director of Christian education for a larger parish, the teacher in weekday religious education, Christian education executive in a council of churches (usually involving co-ordinating and training in children's work, youth work, weekday work, leadership education, and parent education and family life), field service person in Christian education (at the district, state, or national level, or in some specialized form of field service), denominational program building and servicing person at the national level, interdenominational program co-ordinating and servicing person at the national level, writers and editors (curriculum and other), and the teachers of Christian education in college and seminary.

It is entirely possible that the field of leadership training, if it is presented as has been done here by describing a number of kinds of programs designed to further it, will only add up to confusion in the minds of those who are responsible for it in the local church and the local community. Several different policies, which may be in conflict with each other, are involved. No one program could or would use very many of the types of training available. The question of volunteer versus professional leadership remains essentially unanswered. How may a way be found through the confusion and difficulty?

Leadership is a function of the church. Leadership training is basically a matter of making the nature and mission of the church clear, establishing the functions of leadership in light of the nature and mission of the church, and selecting and educating persons to know those functions well and to perform them skillfully. The church is brought into existence and sustained by the gospel, else it is not the church. Leadership training, in all its varied modes, will be effective as it is conducted in the light of the role of the leader in the church of Jesus Christ.

ADMINISTRATION THEORY

Having analyzed and weighed the programs and institutions of Christian education, the field of administration, and the problem and possibilities of leadership, we are at the point where the three questions of administrative theory may be answered and principles of administration suggested.

How and by whom shall the program be organized?

The discussion above suggests an interesting conclusion — that no one type of organization is absolutely essential for Christian education. The requirements are a quality, a concern, and an element of creativity. The required quality for organization is gained when it seeks to be first and foremost a channel for the communication of the gospel. The required concern is that it be functional, that is, ready to add or subtract, build or change, as needs arise and as they take particular forms. The element of creativity is present when the organizational pattern is allowed to take on unusual, unique, and interesting forms that will serve to arrest attention because they succeed in communicating the gospel in new and effective ways. Many types of organization are thus possible and desirable.

The program in the local church should be organized by a committee made up of the most able people in the congregation. The committee derives its authority from the official body of the church. Professional people and volunteers may be in an executive relationship to it.

The committee's task is to find the most functional mode of local organization of the program in light of the gospel. It has been suggested that this may well take the form of broad age-level groups (children's work, youth work, and adult work), each set up in its particular way, supplemented by family activities and an all-church program.

This assures wide participation in the planning of the program and in its leadership, and also assures definite guidance and control toward program unification and attention to emergent needs without falling prey to the irrelevant.

How and by whom shall the program be managed?

The function of management is to run the program effectively. The basic principle of management is that it must be democratic. Democracy in administration implies that decisions will be reached by agreement among those concerned, and that executive responsibility will be placed in the hands of those who are designated to do the managing.

Here there is a clear distinction between determining policy (which is to be democratic in the sense of being arrived at after full and penetrating consideration by all concerned) and the executive implementation of policy (which is to be handled by those appointed to manage and given the power to do so). This does not mean that a group decides policy, and that a manager in a subordinate position then puts that policy into effect. The process requires much closer communication than that. What should happen is that the responsible committee identifies a problem, and after discussing it, asks the executive to formulate and suggest policy on it. This he does, and the committee considers his suggestions, perhaps sending them back for revision in the light of their discussion of them. Finally, policy that both the committee and the executive have hammered out is determined on by the committee, and the executive then begins the process of implementation.

Usually, in Christian education, management is in the hands of the officers of various groups and also in the hands of various superintendents. It should be clear that they must all be in close touch with the committee that is charged with policy-making so that the democratic process may operate effectively.

One of the concerns of the committee, shared by all involved, is that the program may be carried out in the light of the gospel. This implies no particular or rigid mode of operation, but it does provide for that mutual understanding, concern, and trust that serve to undergird and guide the whole process, including all policy-making and all executive operations.

How and by whom shall the program be supervised, that
is, standardized, evaluated, and improved?

Too often the supervisory function has been assumed to
be solely in the hands of those who are professionally
trained in Christian education — the minister or the director of Christian education. Actually the basic principle
of supervision is that it must be co-operative. The church,
seeking with integrity to improve itself, must bring everyone concerned into the process, objectively yet deeply.
Co-operative supervision means that the teacher and
leader desires to improve, seeks skilled help in doing so,
and that the skilled supervisor's position is that of co-
operating in the process. This is a far cry from the arbi-
trary notion of supervision by inspection, but the co-
operative approach is much closer to the real mode of the
church's work.

If standardization is co-operative, it will be a process involving teacher, pupil, superintendent, director, minister,
and committee (or in the case of youth work, officers, advisers, members, director, minister, and committee). But
how can this be done without becoming completely un-
wieldy? The answer may be surprising; it is certainly unusual, though it should not be. We do not start from
scratch in the matter of standards, nor are they as elusive
as they are sometimes thought to be. Our basic standard
is that of the life and work of the church in the light of
the gospel. Furthermore, a great deal of work has been
done, and local groups need not do it all over again, in
suggesting the essential qualities and operations in the
work. Groups ought to digest these, weigh them, and make
the necessary local adjustments, but they need not feel
that theirs is really a pioneering job. The committee, the
minister, and the director can be of inestimable help in

providing the resource material required, and in interpreting this process.

Evaluation is a matter of comparing the situation as it is with the standards, in order to provide a base for improvement. Again, the wider the participation the better, in order that the situation itself may be widely and objectively understood, in order that the standards may be known and accepted, and in order that the need for improvement may be generally recognized and the types of improvement that are required known and agreed on by all concerned.

Improvement means many things — reorganization, expansion of necessary services, the curtailment of unnecessary services, curriculum improvement, improvement of teaching, improvement of facilities, improvement of the amount and quality of participation, leadership training, and much more. This is also a co-operative matter, and must be so by the very nature of the Christian education setup. For improvement really to take place as it should, however, there is need for good executive leadership, especially since standardization and evaluation are so closely involved. The executive's responsibilities are essentially to study the situation, weigh the possibilities, make suggestions, and implement those suggestions in such a way that they may be most expeditiously considered, adopted if they are found to be sound and desirable, and put into effect.

◇

Thus the church may seek to become a more effective channel for the communication of the gospel through its program of Christian education, and may indeed become in its very administration an experience of the gospel in living action. Many people are deeply involved in the experience; as they seek to make their organization really functional in terms of serving its ultimate objective, their management basically democratic, and their supervision broadly co-operative and responsible, they may come close to discovering what it means to be Christ's company doing the educational work of the church.

Conclusion

The Pursuit of Theory

IN THE preceding four chapters a point of view in Christian education has been presented — the outline of a theory that takes the gospel of God's redeeming work in Jesus Christ as its guiding principle.

Some important implications for objectives have been suggested. The analysis of the various functions of objectives showed that the term " objectives " is fraught with ambiguity, that several different types of objectives are spoken of and used, and that the confusion on the matter may be dispelled only when these different types are carefully distinguished from one another in terms of their functions in Christian education. The major finding on objectives, however, was that in the light of the gospel there is primarily one basic objective that provides focus, direction, and selectivity for all Christian education.

The curriculum principles that follow from the guiding principle and the objectives appropriate to it — especially the basic objective — have been outlined. Curriculum was defined as the planned activities through which Christian education may be undertaken. The curriculum principles of comprehensiveness, balance, sequence, and flexibility were examined as to their validity. The problem of the definition of the elements of Christian education led to several suggestions of what those elements might be and how they might be listed, and to the identification of the changing needs and experiences of persons in relation to the other elements as the organizing principle for the curriculum. It was then shown how, with such an understanding of the curriculum, objectives might be used, the curriculum designed and materials built, responsibility assumed for it, and how and by what criteria it might be evaluated. Finally, it was shown how proper use of curriculum materials might be guaranteed.

The principles of administration that appeared to be consonant with the guiding principle were drawn. It was pointed out that administration is a function of the church of Jesus Christ, and that it is thus to be carried on itself in the light of the gospel. The functions of organization, management, and supervision, under the gospel, were shown to lend themselves to the use of functional, democratic, and co-operative principles. The problem of church administration, including the administration of Christian education, was seen to be that of providing the necessary programs and institutions, but at the same time leaving the gospel unfettered by those programs and institutions.

I believe that this constitutes the beginnings of a sound theory of Christian education. Further investigations of the gospel, education, and their implications and relationships are called for, however, in order that the theory may be developed and much needed applications to practice discovered. This has become very evident to me as I have written the various chapters. At many points I have tried to be explicit as to the future investigations that are necessary to develop and examine the principles involved. Further research is required on these and other questions.

Thus, although I have considered it important to present an outline of my convictions on Christian education theory, I have considered it equally imperative to try to stimulate interest in and concern for the building of theory in Christian education by showing what is involved and how it may be accomplished. The need, then, is for the pursuit of theory. The need as presented in this book has been developed in terms of a theory (summarized in the section that follows) that goes deeply into the nature of the culture and education of the particular church.

Essentials in Theorizing About Christian Education

The basic question is whether it is possible to construct a theory of Christian education (a body of basic principles) that will be theologically valid and at the same time educationally sound. The key factor in answering this question is that of modern culture. Today's cultural situation is bringing about radical alterations in our religious life and our educational systems. The culture is extremely heterogeneous, but may be said to be strongly secular and scientific. It tends to approach every aspect of life in a technical and specialized way. This culture is producing profound changes in education. It is also powerfully influencing the theology and life of the church.

Education has been affected by the secular and scientific aspects of the culture in that it has tried hard to become a science, with trained specialists in charge of its planning and operations and with vast networks of institutions for doing its work. The chief results of the pressures that the secular and scientific aspects of the culture have brought to bear upon the thought and life of the church are a technical and professionalized theology and highly organized and promoted church life.

The situation requires a solution that is fundamentally theoretical, since it must take so many factors into account.

The principles that constitute the theory that is required will be adequate and useful only to the extent that they take the cultural situation with the utmost seriousness, reflect the church's life and thought accurately, and take full cognizance of the educational process.

The rank and file of Christian educators have not reached the point of technical and professional understanding (either theologically or educationally) and tend to be bewildered by the aims, procedures, and programs they are supposed to deal with. As a result they adjust themselves as best they can to the situation, usually by conducting their work in ways that would be more suitable in a less complex and more homogeneous culture. Theory, in the sense of a great body of theological and educational principles, does not really promise to give us the answer to our problem in the form in which we most need it.

The solution for us in our present circumstances lies in the refinement of Christian education's body of principles to the point where its particular thrust is unmistakably evident. This means the discovery and use of a guiding principle for Christian education, a focus for its theory that is adequate (that is, theologically and educationally sound) and at the same time so simple and clear that it may be readily grasped, comprehended, and used by the nonprofessional. This would make it possible for everything that is done in planning and carrying on the work of Christian education to be based upon a shared theological understanding, common to professional and nonprofessional alike.

Throughout the history of Christian education, many such guiding principles have been proposed, and systems of Christian education built in terms of them. The advocates of several of the alternatives have in recent decades insistently demanded their recognition and use.

The examination of the claims of these various principles suggests that the most adequate, simple, and clear guide to Christian education is the gospel. As a guiding principle, this means that the central concern of, and norm for, the educational life and work of the church is the gospel — in all its implications for the revelation of God, the nature and condition of man, the meaning of history, individual and social salvation and responsibility, the significance and mission of the church, and the fulfillment of human destiny.

With the gospel at the heart of its educational theory (as the basis for its educational self-understanding) the church may begin to work out the major implications of this principle for the practical side of its educational work. This means the development of a framework of related and consistent principles to guide in the construction of the objectives of Christian education, the construction of educational procedures (curriculum), and the construction of educational programs and institutions (administration). Thus, with the gospel at the center as its basic principle, Christian education will have the guidance of a theory of objectives, a curriculum theory, and a theory of administration.

THE IMPROVEMENT OF THEORY

The improvement of theory in Christian education is a matter of the improvement of theory-making as well as the improvement of the content of theory. Both, as I have pointed out, are greatly needed if an effective practice of Christian education is to have a sound rationale to undergird it.

If, then, the improvement of theory is of such prime importance, how is it to be undertaken? What is required is a new and more serious role for research in Christian education, and a co-ordinated program of research among all those concerned with theory.

Vast and expensive enterprises in Christian education have often been undertaken in the past with little or no research as to their validity or promise. The role of research is twofold: to give the best indication possible as to the grounding and appropriateness of a practical proposal and to predict how well that proposal is likely to meet the need it is intended for. When Christian educators become aware that research can perform these functions, a climate favorable to its increased use will begin to form.

Given a serious role, Christian education research may proceed to perform important services for theory in the improvement of the basic questions that Christian education asks, the formulation of hypotheses to answer these questions, the use of existing and often untapped resources, the development of new resources, and the carrying forward of needed investigations and experiments, all resulting in the formation of a body of tested principles.

A co-ordinated program of research among all those concerned would include the seminaries, colleges, universities, interdenominational groups, and the denominations. The seminaries, colleges, and universities need to move in the direction of establishing research centers for Christian education, promoting co-ordinated individual research and group research in a workshop setting. Their greatest contribution could be in the investigation of the foundations of Christian education, developing them in a systematic, disciplinary fashion. Is it too much to hope that this might eventuate in a mature understanding of the meaning of theology and the church for Christian education, a philosophy of Christian education, a history of Christian education, a psychology and sociology of Christian education, and even a knowledge of the application of communications theory to Christian education? The task involved is that of the formulation and testing of principles of Christian education.

Interdenominational research (making use of research bureaus, laboratories, committee work, and workshop groups) could, on the basis of the work of higher education research centers, proceed to discover the application of the findings to matters of policy, curriculum design, and program construction. Denominational research (working from research bureaus through to the local church itself) could then seek to discover the application of research findings to the detailed problems of construction and use in curriculum and program. A great deal of adjustment to denominational requirements would be called for, but this could be anticipated in the work done in the research centers and by the interdenominational groups. Practical evaluation might very well be made chiefly by denominational groups.

The question of the official status of the findings of research in theory is sometimes raised. Should not church councils make official pronouncements on principles and policy? This may be done under two conditions: first, that the pronouncements represent genuine consensus, and secondly, that provision be made for review and amendment.

More important than such official action, which should certainly be infrequent, is the regular dissemination of findings and proposals through publications and through regional and national meetings. These are needed so that those involved in research may compare notes and be provided the stimulus and direction for the development of their work. Research in the development of Christian education theory is necessarily a joint enterprise demanding the best from everyone concerned.

◇

When the construction of theory is begun on this basis, there remains the responsibility for day-to-day translation of theoretical insights and principles into practice. Theory is devoid of relevance and value unless it is used to guide the church's life and work as it seeks to fulfill the educational demands that are made of it.

Translating theory into practice is a matter of realistic recognition of the pitfalls and hazards that will be encountered, knowledge of the conditions that must be met, and the fashioning of a strategy that promises to accomplish the desired results in the light of these factors. Such a strategy will do well to mind the immediate steps before it with the utmost care, but it cannot do so without stumbling, unless it is determined never to allow itself to lose sight of its long-range imperatives — its theoretical grounding, its guiding principle, its objectives, its curriculum principles, and its principles of administration.

Appendix

Some Objections to the Term "Gospel"

THE question, " Whose gospel? " is often raised as one discusses making the gospel central in Christian education. As one student put it, there are a multiplicity of " true gospels," and the fact that a number of interpretations of the Christian faith confuse the situation makes the use of any one term meaningless.

This presents a problem in the philosophy of religion. Is there a common referent for the different interpretations? If there is, then the use of the term is justified and indeed highly desirable.

The term " gospel " is, of course, sometimes used to mean " something received as absolutely true," or " any doctrine earnestly advocated by its supporters." (*Winston Dictionary,* College Edition.) It is difficult to see how the term as it has been used throughout this discussion (the good news of God's redeeming work in Christ) could be mistaken for its use in connection with these two definitions.

Assuming, then, that the context for the term is Christian and Biblical, are there still a variety of " true gospels " to confuse its use?

There are certainly a number of interpretations of the gospel, and witness to the gospel would seem to be as varied as the number of witnesses. But if that to which the interpretations refer, that to which witness is given, is the good news that God was in Christ reconciling the world to himself, then the referent is a real referent, and the gospel is an actuality, an " existent."

If the gospel is a real referent, there is point and value in the process of creative interpretation that produces different " gospels." If we " witness to" the gospel, the problem of presenting discrete gospels is put in proper perspective. Others also witness; the aim of all of us is that the individual may see and experience the gospel for himself, and join with us in the working and witnessing fellowship of believers. It is Christian education's responsibility to get the pupil into the stream of recognition of the gospel as a real referent, interpretation of it, and belief in it.

◇

Again, there is fear on the part of some that the use of the term " gospel," in any exalted way in Christian education, will simply play into the hands of the revivalists. (I use the word " revivalists " because, although it lacks precision, it will bring to mind exactly the position and type of person referred to.) This, because of the way in which many revivalists have used the idea of the gospel, would mean Christian education's association with an uncritical Biblicism, its failure to see the gospel's relevance to areas of human concern like social responsibility, its acceptance of certain cultural and secular norms and values because the significance of the gospel for their reconstruction has never been explored or has been actively resisted, its being tied up with poor taste in matters of musical standards and the like, and its unexamined use of techniques of mass persuasion. The trouble with the revivalists is that, as they preach the gospel (which for the most part they in fact do), they are also culture-bound but refuse to recognize that fact or do anything about it.

Christian education would be severely handicapped if any of these things happened to it, and they could happen if acceptance of the gospel as its guide were interpreted in a limited sense. But what has actually taken place is that the term " gospel " as the revivalists have tended to use it has represented only one application of its Biblical meaning, and has represented in many cases its virtual betrayal into the hands of the secular culture. The " convert " has been given to believe that his public acceptance of Christ has given him new life (which is perfectly possible) , and that this in turn means the solution of all his and the world's problems (which is not possible) . It has been a major contention of the revivalists, for instance, that the answer to the world's ills is the personal conversion of individuals. It has also been a contention of theirs that a new heart creates new attitudes and dispositions in all life's relationships almost instantaneously. The result all too often has been that the convert has been placed in a position in which he has tried to be a Christian and a secularist at the same time. He has been deluded into thinking that he has rejected the culture, that he is no longer of " this world," because as a Christian he now avoids certain aspects of the life of the world, engages in certain " Christian " cultic practices, and associates with a few of the proper groups and causes. But seldom is he encouraged to face, analyze, think through, and deal with the culture's really profound challenges to the gospel, the church, and the individual Christian. Seldom is it pointed out to him in a realistic way that a lifelong tension, involving difficult and far from clear-cut decisions at many points, is in store for him.

But such a limitation on the work of the gospel and such

a distortion of its meaning and application call only the more insistently, in my judgment, for the unfettering of the gospel of God in Christ so that its redeeming work in its fullest sense may be carried on in the individual life and in the fabric of society. Christian education in the inclusive sense with which it has been described here is in the best possible position to assist theologians, Biblical scholars, and the church in rehabilitating the term " gospel " to the extent that such rehabilitation is needed.

INDEX

INDEX

Action, and social action, 58–59, 61, 110, 122, 130, 137, 138–139, 147, 149, 150, 151, 157, 180–181

Administration, 7, 8, 9, 41, 42, 57, 66–68, 70–71, 72, 74, 76, 77–81, 83, 84, 86, 92, 97, 110, 112, 113, 115, 128, 129, 132, 145, 152–170, 172, 174, 175, 178. *See also* Management; Organization and program; Planning; Supervision

Adults, 46, 117, 149, 153, 157, 160, 166

Age-level objectives. *See* Levels of progress; Sequence

Arts, 18, 26, 34, 149

Authority, 21, 24, 56, 155

Balance, 132, 133, 137, 140, 171

Bible: and curriculum, 62, 88, 92, 122, 136, 147; and a guiding principle, 88, 89–90, 97, 179–181; and revelation, 43–44, 55, 98–105, 148; in the public school, 59; study of, 45, 138, 149. *See also* Word of God

Character, 65, 122

Children, 16, 32, 33, 46, 48, 58, 60, 63, 90, 92, 97, 117, 123, 148, 149, 153, 156, 157, 160, 161, 166

Christian, the: and secularism, 57, 59, 180–182; and his educational needs, 51, 72, 111, 115–116, 117–118, 120, 138–139, 145–146, 172

Christian education: and the church, 42–55, 97–98, 108–112, 115–117, 128–130, 132, 142–143, 145–146, 147–151, 152–170, 172, 173–175; and the cultural situation, 13–14, 21, 27–28, 31, 36–37, 42–55, 56–57, 72, 82–83, 88, 97, 110–111, 113–114, 117–118, 128, 129, 173–175, 180–182; and its practice, 72–81, 83–85, 114, 115–117, 145–146, 172, 175, 178; and its present commitments, 69–70; and its setting, 129; and